SOMATIC AWARENESS

A GUIDE TO RELEASING PATTERNS THAT NEGATIVELY AFFECT OUR EVERYDAY LIFE.

Clifford L. Carter, USNV
INNER WARRIOR SPIRIT founder &
creator of NEUTRALIZING DIS-EASE

Somatic Awareness
A guide to releasing patterns that Negatively affect our everyday life
Neutralizing Dis-Ease Course Material
Clifford L. Carter, USNV
November 2023 ~ First Edition

2023 © All Rights Reserved, *Neutralizing Dis-Ease* is the intellectual property of Clifford L. Carter and may not be copied, distributed, or transferred to any individual or any organization in any form or medium without written permission. Please direct all correspondence regarding the Authorized Curriculum to Clifford L. Carter.

2023 © Images and quotes are the intellectual property of Clifford L. Carter and are not to be reproduced, copied, or distributed in any form or medium.

Without limiting the rights under copyright reserved above, no part of this publication may be reproduced, stored in or introduced into retrieval system, or transmitted, in any form or by any means (electronic, mechanical, photocopying, recording, or otherwise), including mediums not yet invented at time of publication, without prior written permission from both the copyright owner and the publisher of this book.

All images, texts, and copyrighted materials included in this book are the personal property of the author or the author has been given permission to use.

For information regarding permission, email Lionheart Group Publishing: permissions@lionheartgrouppublishing.com

Cover by Sandra Miller

ISBN: 978-1-938505-64-5
Library of Congress Control Number: 2023950233

Companion Course Material to NEUTRALIZING DIS-EASE Mindfulness-Based Authorized Curriculum 2022.

10 9 8 7 6 5 4 3 2 1

Published by Lionheart Group Publishing, Lander, WY, USA~a division of the nonprofit Lionheart Guild, Inc.
Published in the USA ~ All rights reserved.

Visit us on the web at www.lionheartgrouppublishing.com

Acknowledgments

THIS MANUAL HAS BEEN A life-long journey of understanding. This would not have been possible without the many teachers with whom I have been fortunate enough to cross paths.

I also acknowledge the many organizations who have made my journey what it has become, enabling me to put it into words and actions that facilitate growth. I would not have been able to fashion a comprehensive manual that focuses on acceptance through a process of identifying patterns unless I had faced this process myself.

Teachers come in all forms, with or without the label of *teacher*. Experience, when viewed through a lens of openness, can only then allow us to fully take responsibility for our own part in the grand scheme we call *life*.

I also acknowledge those who came before me in that they may take solace in the hope that I might have made a small contribution to their teachings. And to those who will come after as they might gain even one small nugget from what I have learned and shared.

Somatic Awareness

Neutralizing Dis-Ease Course Material

THE PYRAMID OF NEUTRALIZING DIS-EASE

Somatic Awareness

Table of Contents

Introduction xi
1: Assessment 1
2: My Story ~ Trauma 7
3: Experience in Transformation 17
4: Environmental Pollutants 25
5: Meditation Techniques 29
6: Expelling Myths 41
7: Grasping & Aversion 45
8: Brain Science 51
9: Clinging & Craving 61
10: Dependent Origination 67
11: Questioning Mind 75
12: Radical Acceptance 81
13: Seeing and Seeing Deeply 91
14: Dis-Ease 101

15: Remedy...105

16: Our Mind is Not Its Own..............................111

17: Fixed & Movable...121

18: Understanding Consciousness....................127

19: Troubleshooting...131

20: Afterward..135

About the Author..141

"Who we are starts on the inside and slowly works its way to the surface."

SOMATIC AWARENESS
NEUTRALIZING DIS-EASE COURSE MATERIAL

COURSE OVERVIEW REVIEW

AFTER THREE DECADES OF MINDFULNESS practice, and more than ten years of developing and teaching *Neutralizing Dis-Ease* to hundreds of participants, I created this curriculum with the hope that others can follow the life-changing approach to mindfulness using insight meditation. As we go through eleven weeks of classroom structure, we learn about pairing mindfulness meditation, senses, and how the mind works for and against us at every turn.

Insight meditation is simply seeing within. We will be seeing within, and also noticing sensations both inside and outside our body, using our breath as the stable and mind-calming effect it has on one's nervous system. In addition to the thinking mind, we'll learn how to observe our six senses without getting attached to or detached from one of the senses.

We'll also learn to bring the practice to our world, as any great practice should translate into our daily life. Without a translation, we become tied to our space at home—quiet, calm, structured, etc. That's not how the world truly is for most of us. I bridge that gap by starting on the cushion, creating what I call 'sitting with our uncomfortableness', then expanding the practice into the world.

The effects of the practice of mindfully going through each sense is truly transformational. By the end of eleven weeks, you'll have become aware of your true nature by way of your senses, in a way you have yet to comprehend.

As an observer, we have the opportunity to sit without judgment: good, bad, happy, sad. We are simply experiencing a moment in time, truly accepting just as we are.

"Accepting who we are
in this moment in time
is the way to truly let go
of the mindless acts
that hold us
to this existence."

Clifford L. Carter

Somatic Awareness

Neutralizing Dis-Ease Course Material

(I)

Assessment

First when assessing, we must be clear about what the *problem* actually is.

From my view, the problem is suffering and how we come to this place of feeling less than we believe we should. By teasing apart suffering, we must look at our perception of suffering and what holds us back from viewing suffering as pleasurable—or some place between pleasure and pain. Is suffering something we experience physically and/or mentally? Is it something that comes from people, places, and things? Might suffering be generated by our own perception of external factors?

Those all contribute to a feeling of incorrectness of what our focus is on in any given moment. Then does it become the focus on a feeling or event that brings suffering? And why not shift focus to end the painful experience?

That's what we might think of as having our heads in the sand.

The question becomes, "How long can we keep our head in the sand without taking our next breath?"

Can it be that our beliefs cause suffering, and the way to end suffering is simply to find a new narrative to believe in?

It's not so simple to change narrative, because the idea of how we see ourselves and how we would like others to see us is the very thing that not only defines us but generates a feeling of safety. In that, anything counter to our narrative could be threatening to our existence.

Now that we have explored the idea perception as a key factor in exposing a problem, let's go deeper into perception.

The clearest understanding of pain and suffering is attachment to our perception. It is the need to define in various degrees what is right and wrong for us. The need to be right or feel a certain way creates a need facilitated by a sense of safety. From where did that sense of safety and the very need for safety come?

When addressing a problem facilitated by perception, we must also consider the cause and how we have come to *the labeling* of the very thing happening as what we describe as *problem.*

Problem is something that may not feel right. It is something that goes against our understanding of right and wrong, good and bad, pleasure and pain. It is not the idea that a thing is *this* or *that.* The energy surrounding our perception creates solidity in our understanding of an issue.

When the understanding of our environment is challenged, we hold on to it—becoming stuck or fixed without flexibility. Those fixed ideas become our identity.

As our identity continued to solidify over time, it was no longer the idea that caused the problem but the solidity. Imagine feeling tension in one's shoulders. If not addressing the cause, the tension becomes stronger and stronger as if it would never pass, becoming more and more firm. It was the cause, or the underlying condition, that manifested tension in the first place. If we look past the tension to what was behind the solidity, we find the cause. In most cases, behind that cause we find yet another cause that continues all the way back to birth.

While addressing trauma, it is the very idea that the event was not supposed to happen at all. Free from value, the tendency is to push the experience away. Thus, only learning to push painful experiences away—again burying one's head in the sand.

> "Always grasping outside in an attempt to understand internal struggles seems backward, but it is human nature to believe we alone, are not enough."

If our normal from birth was experiencing events and circumstances surrounding those events were described as simply part of everyday life without question, no negative charge would exist, unless, at some future point, we shifted our belief that disabled the normality of a past experience.

Somatic Awareness ~ Assessment

> As I grew up in the Midwest, my family hunted and fished to provide food and a small amount of income, in addition to my father working shift work at the local ammunition factory. From an early age, hunting and killing animals became my normal.
>
> As I grew up in that environment, those activities became part of my life experience. It was only after I started school and learned from others that I began questioning my *own* reality.
>
> Comparing myself to others and considering an alternative, it eventually became a choice to later disdain the killing I had been raised and acclimated at an early age.

* * *

To accept our narrative is to let go of the idea that that narrative might be flawed and had power over us to a point we become defined as a person formed by circumstance.

What does it take to reform one's narrative?

First, accepting circumstance and understanding we were malleable, absorbing our surroundings without questioning.

The business of inner transformation is hard work. That's why avoidance has become such big business. Using various tactics including sex, overworking, and fishing can be useful avoidance strategies. Temporary fixes leave us numb for the time it takes to bait and reel in a big fish. Usually, as the story goes, much bigger than it really was, anyway. Imagine if as much time were spent on inner transformation as is on avoiding.

Meeting suffering head on without distraction, without narrative, simply being with, accepting, and moving on—that is the work of somatic awareness, facilitated by mindfulness meditation.

"Feeling trauma to the bone is the way transformation takes place, not only on the surface but from the depths of our souls."

Clifford L. Carter

SOMATIC AWARENESS
Neutralizing Dis-Ease Course Material

(2)

My Story/Trauma

TRAUMA STRING

Trauma is like a string forever connected to the victim—a string that has a constant tug. A pulling toward a thing, not even aware how the next approaching will further solidify one's negative feelings.

Alone, abandoned, shame, guilt—all feelings conjured up to justify self-loathing.

That string, however thin or thick, weak or strong, runs all the way back to birth—when breath filled our lungs for the first time and the path of life was entered. The string connects mommy, daddy, sister, brother.

Tugging. Pulling this way and that. Do this. Do that. Be this. Be that. Soon the strand grew, adding grandmother, grandfather, aunt, uncle, cousin. Tugging, pulling, shaming, guilting.

Where is the string connected?

When the cord was cut, a string replaced it—an invisible string with the capacity to hold much firmer than any umbilical cord formed through mother during conception. It is a string—a string of circumstance that later became a string of destiny, of choice, and then a string of self defining that could lead to self destruction.

> "Transform begins with letting go. Yes, that means we get to start over."

BIRTH

Dragged out of mother's birth canal two weeks early at nine-and-a-half pounds—a trauma memory still trapped within my body's DNA. Growing up, hearing stories about how big I was and mother's inability to carry me full term.

Mother stood 5'1", approximately 110 lbs. She would often say, "Dynamite comes in small packages."

I later realized the truth in that statement.

As years passed, a feeling that something very wrong had happened when I came into this world—a feeling of dis-ease, unprepared for what was to come.

Fifty years later, I questioned mother about my birth and the step-by-step details.

At first, she stated it was an easy birth. After my brother, I came right out.

I said, "You always said I was two weeks early and nine-and-a-half pounds."

"Yes, but the birth was easy."

"So, tell me step by step. I know something happened. I can still feel it inside me that my birth was a traumatic event."

Mother went on to say they took her into a room, put her feet up in stirrups, and gave her no birth inducing medication.

Rather, the doctor put his hand inside her and broke her water.

The moment she said the doctor put his hand inside her, I had a flashback of the experience. Not in a literal sense but in a body memory. My whole physical being tensed up and cold chills ravished my body from head to toe, followed by sobbing tears.

I had not wanted to come out. That was the message that kept repeating through my mind like and airplane pulling a banner behind.

"Where does this come from?" I asked myself.

It was a body memory trapped for so long deep in my DNA that pulled and pushed to get out. My mind had dreamt up a story to keep me safe.

Feeling like that was simply being born without question, without an act or action, contrary to belonging to this world or that.

* * *

My body and my mind finally collided with truth. Feeling and thought connected in a way that not only showed me the real truth but allowed me in some small way to heal from, or at the very least acknowledge the happening and move on to the next sensations arising.

Trust the body, become aware of the task of the mind, and start to free oneself.

AWARENESS AND DEPRESSION/ALONENESS

Awareness in and of itself is the focus on a thing or object. That may seem as simple as placing one's attention on a sight or a sound, a tree, or even a feeling or thought.

For the purpose of this exploration, awareness has been placed on the feeling of depression and aloneness.

I ask myself first and even wonder from where does the feeling of depression and aloneness come? Where does it reside? What is the nature and what is the quality of the feeling?

I cling to a thing not only because it may feel good but because it may feel familiar—because it is how I have defined myself—how I have seen myself in this world based on past experiences I have accepted as my truth.

When opportunities arise in my daily life that facilitate a belief I hold or cling to, the depressive alone transports me to a past time—a time long past, but it continues to shadow the gift of today and tomorrow.

Sitting in meditation as sensations arise, entering in to *the Mind Space* to be decided—good, bad, neutral, cling, let go, or simply observe. The process of the human mind acts out moment to moment, time and time again, solidifying whom I believe myself to be through my pain and suffering and through everyone and everything I have ever met and ever even thought or felt about.

Be with, accept, and let go.

Be open—so open that all passes through, nothing gets stuck.

Nothing and no one decides who I am.

The 'who I am' has always been who I am.

My only job is to come back home, come back to my true nature—the nature I was born with before the world was placed on my shoulders.

* * *

<u>BONE</u>

Trauma broke the wings off my inner warrior spirit.

Choked this life-less body and left it for dead.

Running, running, running—with no connection to pain.

Feeling only torture, turmoil, upset, and rage.

Trauma broke the wings off my inner warrior spirit.

Choked this life-less body and left it for dead.

I can only see a world filled with illusion and strange.

Filling my life with confusing restraint.

Trauma broke the wings off my inner warrior spirit.

Choked this life-less body and left it for dead.

I'm never gonna climb to that mountain top.

I'm never gonna have a life of my own.

Trauma broke the wings off my inner warrior spirit.

Choked this life-less body and left it for dead.

I wish I was faster

I wish I was stronger

I wish I was wiser

If I only had friends and not been alone

Always alone, Always alone

Trauma broke the wings off my inner warrior spirit.

Choked this lifeless body and left it for dead.

* * *

I JUST DON'T KNOW IF I CAN STAY

THOUGHTS OF SUICIDE

I sit here with tears running down my face.

What has this world become?

No one cares about death and destruction.

Only building walls.

Walls from the outside.

Walls so deep and wide our own self has become abandoned from hope of ever returning.

I just don't know if I can stay

Why do we hate so much and feel so little?

How do we see when we are blind?

When can the tragedy outside eliminate the pain we feel on the inside?

I just don't know if I can stay

Agenda, Agenda, Agenda

We all have one.

Self preservation at any cost.

At the cost of another.

At the hands of few, many or our own.
Makes no difference anymore.
I just don't know if I can stay

Hopelessness, fear, and isolation.
Suicidal ideation.
Misunderstanding.
The world keeps spinning.
People keep dying.

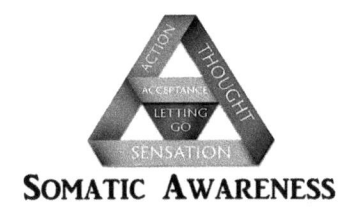

Somatic Awareness

NEUTRALIZING DIS-EASE COURSE MATERIAL

(3)

Experience in Transformation

As SOMATIC AWARENESS UNFOLDS, WE begin to experience self by revealing our true nature in a way that gently sheds light on understanding necessary for a transformational path. Being present in the moment, experiencing the sensations of the body and mind, we can begin to notice threads of commonality—ways of thinking and being in the world.

Those willing to open themselves up to the process of seeing clearly in the moment, without judgment, can and will have clarity into the strands that tug and pull originating from all past experience to this very day and time.

"Endless strands with one true unchanging core so connects us all."

The question becomes, "Are we ready and willing to explore 'The who I have become'?"

Somatic Awareness ~ Experience in Transformation

My own transformation started as a child with questioning my surrounding, being curious how and why my parents related to each other in a certain way at a certain time. What we had for dinner, why, including the texture, temperature, sweet or salty flavor along with detecting seasonings as they became more and more familiar.

Moving on to the idea of right and wrong, good and bad, pleasure and pain. Those would be the attachments that moved me to the person I would become.

Holding on to ideas, giving effort used to cling on to the concepts that formed my person.

The holding on to and the willingness to cling until it became physically impossible to do so caused my pain and suffering. How long was I able to hold a ball compared to how long I was able to hold a thought originated from my feelings of value. In a sense, holding a ball on the surface has little to do with self worth.

On the other hand, holding on to a feeling about self or the concept of rightness has long-lasting consequence, further solidified by the mind. In this scenario, thinking takes place in the vacuum of one's own mind—taking little consideration of any other possibility that may be offered by current circumstance, either presented by another or simply waiting patiently for our distraction.

The very distraction that cuts, in a sense, the cord that binds one to past ideals—the awareness that many events happen simultaneously in a given moment, opens the possibility that change is infinite. Same as, possibilities are infinite, and focusing on a concept as holding a ball narrows the mind.

Expanding the mind enables us to allow concepts outside our own patterning. For me, that came in the form of curiosity. Not knowing is the key to letting go if we are willing to see and experience life from the lens of a child.

That was one of the most challenging concepts for me to grasp. The idea I might not know, I might not be right—that it might be helpful to explore the scary thing that lives outside my developed consciousness.

As I pushed myself outside my sense of comfort, I gained an understanding of what was true and also what might not be serving me so well in each moment.

I remember, shortly after I joined the US Navy, making a pact with myself about experiencing food from places I would visit.

Growing up in southern Illinois, meat, potatoes, and river fish had been staples, so I figured food was a way to immerse myself in other cultures. From head-on eyes staring at me, crayfish soup in Guam, to simple artichokes in Connecticut opened my mind to infinite possibilities outside the diet with which I had growing up.

I did not realize that had been a strategy which allowed me to find joy in the unknown—a way to step outside myself and into a world of awe and wonder. As If I were tasting peas and carrots from a short screw-top glass jar, narrated by mother.

Time went on and curiosity moved from food to most any circumstance I could muster up the courage to undertake.

Looking back at those times and the expansive way I moved through the world, compared to the narrowing of my mind compounded by a traumatic event, got me exploring a way back.

For me, the way back from a traumatic event was not to relive the event, but examine the edges. Examining the edges is like moving over, around, under, and sometimes through an obstacle with full awareness.

Using my five senses and *the Thinking Mind* in each moment to explore with curiosity rather than known, trusted ideas, allowed me to get close enough. It became the subtly for what I did not know I would focus on—leaving the solid ideas aside for a time.

Today, as life still gets bigger than me from time to time, I use the tools of mindfulness—the idea that whatever is happening in the moment will shift into another thing. What happens in my mind will also transform into some new and different thought, generated by a sensation or no obvious sensation at all.

My mind has the capacity to expose a thought without sensation.

Intrusive thoughts come and go unless there is an attachment. Clinging to a thought further solidifies the same thinking and same being.

* * *

> I met a hound dog when I was in treatment for PTSD years ago at the Topeka, Kansas VA Medical center.
>
> She happened to be the same breed I was raised with 'coon hunting on the Mississippi river bottoms.

I visited her every week, and when she went to the vet for a surgery I had a panic attack. I told the pet shop how much she meant to me, and they wanted to give her to me.

The problem was, a lot of strings attached to that giving. Every time the pet shop owner pulled a string, I felt trauma increase, and every time I let go, trauma relaxed.

That dog taught me the power trauma had over me and how trauma had previously pushed me to attempt taking my life three times. She taught me the power of letting go. In the end, I let go of her because she had done what she came into my life to do—she taught me a very valuable lesson. The power of letting go.

* * *

Now, I try my best to share the tools of mindfulness meditation practice that starts with the breath and ends with letting go, mindfully working with the five sensations and the mind.

What a profound experience, nudged by a dog.

MUSHROOM

Cause and Effect by Way of the Morel Mushroom

I've recently been mushroom hunting without any luck. People say morels are hard to find. The last trip I made, I finally found a patch of morels. Mother nature creates the causes (spring soil warmed by the sun on a south facing hillside) and the effects are morels, May-apples, fiddlehead ferns, Jack-in-the-pulpits popping up everywhere. Green moss carpets the ground under an early morning dew.

How fortunate we humans are to have the ability to understand the law of cause and effect. If we can see the causes we are about to affect, we can begin to drive our destiny in a direction that will ultimately reach a place of peace. Of course, we have choice.

I believe if we can look at an effect and trace it backwards, we can learn the cause. When we see the cause connected to a negative effect, then we have clear choice. Sometimes we get stuck making bad choices even if we understand the effects of those choices.

Sometimes I get stuck and sometimes I make good choices...

* * *

ON LOVE

Why does the obstacle of love show up in the form of distance, health, physical attraction, education, income, etc.

The heart knows no sensation other than feeling.

Feelings know none of the above ideas placed in the mind through the eyes, ears, nose, mouth, and touch.

Yet we give credence to the mind nearly 100% of the time, disregarding the true self that leads us to our best self and allows us to become the whole self we were intended to be from the very start.

"Accepting who we are in this moment in time is the way to truly let go of the mindless acts that hold us to this existence."

Clifford L. Carter

Somatic Awareness
Neutralizing Dis-Ease Course Material

(4)

Environmental Pollutants

DEFINED AS: PEOPLE, PLACES, THINGS—EVERYTHING IN AND AROUND US WE DIRECTLY AND INTENTIONALLY IDENTIFY, IMMEDIATELY WITH A SENSE OF KNOWING. THE KNOWING GENERATES RIGHT, FOLLOWED BY SAFE, OR UNSAFE, DEPENDING ON OUR PATTERNING.

WHO WE HAVE BECOME, BASED on a set of guidelines and framework played out by generational patterns, accepted, and believed to be true or false, gives way to a structure informed by our environment.

Generations of conflict and ease solidify those patterns we call our way of life, culture, circumstance, willingness to conform—if only to feel a sense of belonging or simply a feeling of safety or fear when a situation arises.

From birth to death, ideas define our existence and become solidified by the need to be right. That need for rightness, at its core, stems from a deeper need to feel safe.

Somatic Awareness ~ Environmental Pollutants

As a child explores their world and discovers the sky color to be blue, and later colors the sky blue only to find a peer (being poorly marked with the same landscape and the same choices) with a sky colored brown, green, purple, or even red. That experience only solidifies the sky color must be, in fact, blue. Any deviation clearly would be wrong.

> "Our dependency on rightness originated lifetimes ago linked by the very need to feel safe."

From the moment the sky became blue, the child became right, safe, and better than his or her peer. That certainty gave way to the feeling we must adhere to the rules laid out by our parents and teachers. As time passed, anyone who colored the sky outside the prescribed lines must be wrong and therefore *unsafe*.

The mind begins to close and form how we see the world through a lens of right and wrong based on patterning, solidified by the validating and invalidating actions of our environment.

The simple experience of seeing the sky blue can easily be translated into a vast number of concepts. It is not, however, the actual color of the sky that will later become the stuck point. But rather the idea there's a right and a wrong way. Anyone who challenges beliefs about that idea may be unsafe.

While anyone who adheres to the idea of rightness and wrongness conversely *is* safe and *is* acceptable as friend and ally. The middle, or gray area, in any situation becomes a place of fear and further validates the need to be right. That rightness and wrongness is far from being *okay*. The need to inherently choose a side comes from the need to color the sky blue.

When faced with a decision, the natural choice is to search our past experiences for information that can inform a possible outcome. That process closes any possibility of an outcome free from past patterns, again disabling the possibility to expand our consciousness further from the environmental pollutants that have informed our past.

It is all too easy to move through the world seeing, tasting, touching, smelling, hearing, and thinking based on patterns that brought us here. Growth does not happen when we follow, but rather when we seek out the uncomfortable.

Explore the boundaries of your patterns and question everything.

In the essay above, *Trauma String*, we followed the concept of generational trauma and how the patterns of that trauma have lifelong consequences.

Somatic Awareness
Neutralizing Dis-Ease Course Material

(5)

Meditation Techniques

The idea there are good and bad meditation techniques is simply a reflection of our own patterning. The idea our meditation practice is correct and therefore is the most useful to us and others, regardless of reaching a state of awakening or Nirvana is detrimental to growth.

Through many years of my own practice of meditation, I have experienced a multitude of techniques. Trial and retrial of those techniques have brought me to a place of rest.

The intention of most meditation practice is to reside in a state of peace.

In my experience, meditation has been translated from source (The Buddha) to what fits a current need.

Need has a grasping nature—a pulling toward self in the idea an outside influence can somehow make us feel whole and at peace—much like at school or religious structure where the teacher feeds information to the participants in an attempt to create a certain reality.

That comes from ignorance and the feeling we are not whole or good enough just as we are. The truth is, we have all the answers to all the questions that arise inside ourselves. We can look at that as if we have forgotten or have lost trust in our *true* selves.

Meditation, in its pure form, is about slowing the mind and calming the nervous system so we might see the world as it truly is—free from past pattering that disconnects us from our true nature.

Counting breaths, guided meditation, chanting, mudras, imagination, and many other types of meditation practices can be useful in the moment. They often lead us in a circle back to where we started, with enough relaxation that brings us back for more.

It's a useful trap—not only for the ego but for the developer of the practice on which we become stuck.

Those practices are simply adding to the moment without accepting what has already taken place. The idea of adding becomes a distraction for what is happening in the moment, instead of allowing sensations to naturally arise and fall.

When we use our breath as our focus, or stability, our breath becomes the anchor to self and enables one to clearly see what is happening in the moment— the happening we call *mindfulness*. The only way to enter mindfulness in the moment is by focusing on the breath, without outside implements or concepts that evade our awakening.

Mindfulness is the seeing or being with an experience or object in a much deeper way. That deep experience allows us to subtly shift our ideas about the experience and re-explore it from a slightly different lens.

There are some myths about each person's ability to meditate. A common myth might be, "I cannot meditate because my mind never stops thinking."

The idea *the Thinking Mind* never stops is correct—much like seeing, tasting, touching, smelling, and hearing. Ask yourself if there was ever a time you stopped hearing.

We might plug the ears with cotton or put sound-deadening earphones on, and still we hear. That tells us hearing never really stops. The same can be said for the other four senses, and including *the Thinking Mind*.

What changes is the shift in awareness. We become aware of the sensation of touch through a cold breeze on our face, and in the next moment the sound of water, and in the next a thought arises of future planning.

> "Meditation becomes the tool that facilitates inner transformation. As we explore sensation we begin to realize the who we have become is no longer attached to our true nature thus shifting our reality."

In the instant a sensation arises, it is processed by *the Thinking Mind*, which feels like thinking is always happening. There is, of course, something that happens before thinking starts—subtle sensation through our five senses. *The Thinking Mind* has the capacity to generate thoughts without phenomena, referred to as *intrusive thought.*

Intrusive thought is simply ideas arising without the catalyst from seeing, tasting, touching, smelling, or hearing.

The truth is, when we simply notice the breath at any moment we are meditating. We can also focus on the breath and become aware of our surroundings at the same time. That is mindfulness in the moment and the processing of that same information from a slowed mind and calm nervous system.

That facilitates the ability to generate curiosity—questioning any response we might have about our surroundings and enabling us to accept and let go.

THE HIDDEN TRUTH

Human beings doing... What is life about?

Why are we here? What is our purpose?

Those are some of the questions I ask myself every day. When I look at other humans doing, I wonder if the purpose of our existence is simply to do when we are, in fact, called human beings. What if the word *being* itself is a clue into our purpose—our reason for life itself?

We are born, and *being* seems to be the thing we do best. We lay around seeing, tasting, touching, smelling, and hearing the world. Not much interest in doing—simply observing evaluating and wondering. That sounds like *being* to me.

Later, *the Thinking Mind* comes online, learning how to use the other senses' information. That's when the doing begins—whether manipulating others to do for us or we begin to do for ourselves, forming the ego mind—the 'how we see ourselves in the world' and 'how we want others to see us'. The ego mind, along with environmental pollutants, form 'who we will become' and 'how we interact' in our world.

As we now know, environmental pollutants are defined as people, places, and things—the influences we hear, see, touch, taste, and smell, agree with, and become our truths. Those experiences frame our ego, our belief system about ourselves, and how we want others to see and know us.

What if we could be human beings while doing?

* * *

There is a way to go back to the child-like state of being as an adult. We might think of that as going to a playground or finger painting as such. I am speaking of something much deeper than that—something not of the mind. Something not of the surface because, to literally travel to that place is not to use the system that took us far away from our human *being* and left us as only a human *doing*.

The key is found in the simplest of places. It regulates life and death it activates at the same moment our other five senses flood the body.

That should give some indication how important our five senses are, in addition to 'the key'.

The key is *the breath.* The combination is our senses. Most of us lock the door to understanding self when we begin to use *the Mind.* Even though we do not fully understand *the Mind,* and never really do understand the true nature of *the Mind* and its capacity for clinging and craving.

> *"Good, bad... Pleasure, pain... Their centers bring me comfortably seated between grasping and aversion."*

That nature is the very thing that moves us ever further away from the true self that connects us to all understanding. Not just understanding of self, but the nature of true self and the nature of all existence of the world—self and those traveling in our plane of existence.

The way back to the understanding of *the Mind* is a journey. That journey is dependent on multiple factors. How much we cling to *the Mind* and its usefulness, how much we trust our true nature, how strong our ego state has become, and if we have solid fixed ideas of self.

How do we experience the world and our interaction with our interdependent nature with regard to others?

Using the key, focusing on the key, and becoming aware of the combination as if it were a lock awaiting being opened.

Lifetime after lifetime, if only we could enter and stay as child navigating with our mind, unwilling to accept 'the who we have become' based on the input of others.

If only we could have choice, awe, and wonder to navigate our world with a viewfinder of open expansive clarity that only comes from not knowing, and grows into questioning, observing, and accepting.

The breath is the key and the five senses become the combination to the way back to self—true self, true understanding of who we really are. The body is a temple that only we have access to, with the key and correct combination.

The temple, when correctly accessed, becomes a place of worship. Worshiping inside of self is the true spiritual experience we all strive for—we all search for.

The usual way of searching is generated from the mind. So, naturally we look outside self with the understanding we have gained our whole life from others. That is the way the mind becomes distracted and searching. It keeps us on trail after trail, in circles, looking for answers to questions that cannot be answered. Because the information in our mind comes from others. It does not belong to us. It is not of our temple.

How could that be the way back home?

It is a map of never-ending consequences, leading to nowhere and everywhere the others have already been, and where others before them have already gone. It becomes a cycle of birth, rebirth, circle after circle, time and time again.

The key is the breath, combination of the senses, the temple, the body.

That is the hidden truth that lies right in front of our faces.

RAIN MEDITATION USING EYE SENSATION

Sitting under a watershed, focusing on my breath. Gently opening my eyes encouraged through ear as the drops of water ever stronger and stronger a top the corrugated fiberglass shed roofing.

Eyes seeing a single drop of water as it falls from the sky. From a cloud, questioning where this drop might have come from. How did this single drop of water happen to be, right here right now?

As this droplet of water passes my sight, I cannot help to wonder what is inside this single drop of water. What is it made up of? Where will it land and where will it go?

Hitting the ground with the force so great that this single drop explodes into thousands of smaller droplets of water.

I continue focusing on my breath and go deeper into the path of water through my eyes into my mind, opening all possibilities. Seeing through awe and wonder like the eyes of a child.

* * *

From one drop to hundreds of droplets of water onto the earth, nourishing the smallest plant, animal, and organism. Now this one single drop of water is part of so many others and as the others grow and grow they become part of even more.

An example of natures, *Dependent Origination*. One thing sets off a chain of events that has no beginning and has no end. It is infinite in nature and cannot be started or stopped. We are merrily entering into observing at any set point on the continuum of life's greatest mystery. Which if understood correctly is no mystery at all. Meditation practice using only the breath and questioning mind opens a pathway to understanding.

THE BREATH IS MY TEACHER

> Today, I look out across the canyon and see the yucca. Seemingly unchanged but still something is different. As I explore this different state of being in the world of the yucca it does occur to me the difference may not lie with the yucca at all but within myself. For I see this lonely yucca day after day, stilling the canyon rim without a notice of its ever changing nature.
>
> The breath, my breath becomes the portal—the way into understanding of the who I am at this moment in time. Without the past. Without the future. Pure self and pure understanding of my nature and the relationship with all things.
>
> The breath is the teacher. The breath when focused upon and awareness of a sensation

or sensations becomes my classroom of deep understanding.

Change occurs with or without my notice. Holding onto becomes the struggle. Letting go become the understanding.

The yucca simply breaths in and breaths out. Accepts the water given. The soil it's born into. The light it receives, lives, and dies.

CAN I BE LIKE THE YUCCA?

* * *

Beautiful Meditation

Breath in, Breath out.

Feeling the warm sun on my face. Listening to the breeze blowing through the canyon while occasionally the sound of a bird, the chime of a nearby copper tube, and the rustling of newly fallen leaves.

The mind slows and sensations awaken to surroundings external and then internal sensations connecting me to my true nature. Sorting, sensing, accepting, letting go, and moving on to the next sensation arising.

* * *

Can it be that is life's lesson in just one sit? One connects with self?

Be with, accept, let go, move on to next sensation arising.

"Letting go is as easy as farting, and yet we hold on to it so nobody knows or gets offended."

Clifford L. Carter.

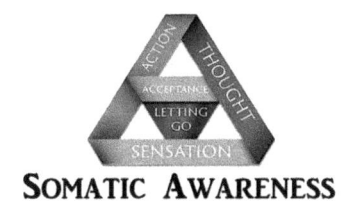

SOMATIC AWARENESS
NEUTRALIZING DIS-EASE COURSE MATERIAL

(6)

EXPELLING MYTHS

CAN THE MIND BECOME STILL, AND IS THAT THE DESTINATION AT ALL?

THAT IS ONE OF THE questions that pops up when people attempt a meditation practice. There are *YouTube* videos that promise still and calm after attempting a certain technique, as long as that specific technique is correctly followed.

Experiencing mantra (chanting a phrase over and over) with the hope the mind becomes still, followed by relaxation, and a deep meditative state is counter to stilling the mind. It is simply distracting the mind.

Counting one, two, three, four, up to ten or twenty, rinse and repeat, is yet another way to distract the mind by giving the mind something to focus on rather than thoughts themselves.

Back to the idea the mind becomes still at all—the truth about *the Mind* is that its job is to think just as the eyes' job is to see, as well as the ears, nose—taste, and touch. *The Thinking Mind* is the sixth sense that has the capacity to generate intrusive thoughts—that is thinking without any input from the other five senses.

Closing one's eyes does not stop the sensation of seeing. The same is true with taste, touch, smell, and hearing. In meditation, as well as outside our sitting practices, our awareness moves from sensation to sensation, attempting to find some reference to which we can attach. The reference is found in what I call *the mind space*. It's like a dictionary of all our past experiences that stores information into categories.

> "It's all around us.. All of the answers to all of your questions are no further than your six senses."

When accessed by *the Thinking Mind*, attachment is formed through the idea that, "I know what that is. I have experienced that person, place, or thing before."

It is not what some would call *déjà vu*. It is an actual account of a past experience that has a predetermined consequence, based on information we have stored for future reference in order to keep us safe—like touching a red-hot stove as a child, forever solidifying that experience so as not to repeat it.

Stored experiences are not all negative. They are also positive, as well as neutral, meaning there is little to no attachment to them.

Once we understand the mind is yet another sense, we realize that visualizing a beach and the warm sand between our toes is simply placing an experience into the mind. It becomes the opposite of stilling or quieting the mind.

As we sit in meditation, focusing on the breath, becoming aware of sensation, and understanding the mind is yet another sensation, we can then allow thoughts to come and go in the same manner we notice we are hearing, seeing, tasting, touching, and smelling. Be with sensation, accept sensation, and move on to the next sensation arising. That's the process of stilling the mind—by way of accepting the mind is thinking and allowing the mind to think without attachment.

If we have a thought and attempt to push it away, we attach to the idea we are not correctly meditating. Allowing the thoughts to come and go by accepting, we are thinking and moving on to another sensation that might be happening in the next moment allows us to become free of attachment to any sensation arising in any given moment.

Thus, allowing the mind to rest in stillness while moving from one sensation to the next and allowing our other senses to rest. That resting is facilitated by slowing the mind and calming the nervous system through the practice of focusing on the breath.

To recap, *the Thinking Mind* in meditation is defined as a sensation no different than our other five senses.

"If we desire change, the simplest way is to do the opposite of what we normally do in the present. The future will then begin to bear fruit of a new consequence."

Clifford L. Carter

Somatic Awareness
Neutralizing Dis-Ease Course Material

(7)

Grasping & Aversion

Grasping and aversion, from the beginning, warrants a breakdown into two equal parts, exhibiting the same force placed in opposing directions.

The idea is that two opposite values have the same energy—a pushing away, and a pulling toward. That generates dis-ease, a belief that we are alone or too much or too little.

The qualities observed within sensation that generate a feeling of grasping could arise in seeing blue sky and open space from the sense of the eyes even with the eyes closed. That sensation is a construct of a past experience, generated by the mind to bring about peace.

All senses have the capacity to generate grasping outside the body as well as inside the body. Internal grasping might be generated by a feeling of the floor beneath our feet or seat that gives a grounding sensation. We are firmly planted and immovable in that moment when our previous world might have looked to be in chaos.

The trap, however, is that we may reach or grasp for that very experience each time we attempt our meditation practice. Entering meditation with that intention surely will give rise to grasping and a feeling of chaos will surely follow.

As we understand our meditation practice and how it relates to grasping, we can easily translate that into our daily lives by realizing our very nature is to reach for what feels good and expect that will serve us well into the future. Only then can we clearly see grasping for something we do not have in that moment only causes more grasping, which leads to an endless cycle of pain and suffering.

WHY ARE WE SO AFRAID OF SELF?

As previously stated, the business of inner transformation is hard work. That must be why avoidance has become so lucrative—avoidance strategies including drugs, alcohol, porn, vacation, fishing, hiking, camping, boating—even grocery shopping... You get the point that avoiding self can take on any form to which we can attach so we don't feel the self.

When pain and suffering arise, the tendency is to push it away by using any number of strategies—creating a temporary fix—checking out when the very remedy is checking in. Just think if the cost and simplicity of inner transformation—real inner transformation—was free.

Is that too simple?

Is that too free?

Perhaps.

* * *

Aversion is 'the pushing away from' a sense that may feel uncomfortable. It is sometimes described as 'red' or 'fire' from the eye sense and touch sensation. Both are generated from outside the body, and both are constructs from past experience that tells us red and fire are things of which we should be fearful. That fear, or dis-ease, generates a pushing away energy.

Inside the body, aversion is generated by sensations we might routinely call *pain*. They are feelings of tightness, warmth, coolness while scanning the body. When we label a sensation painful or pleasurable, we close the mind to a deeper experience.

Past patterning gives rise to our understanding of pain and pleasure in a way we no longer choose to have a deeper experience.

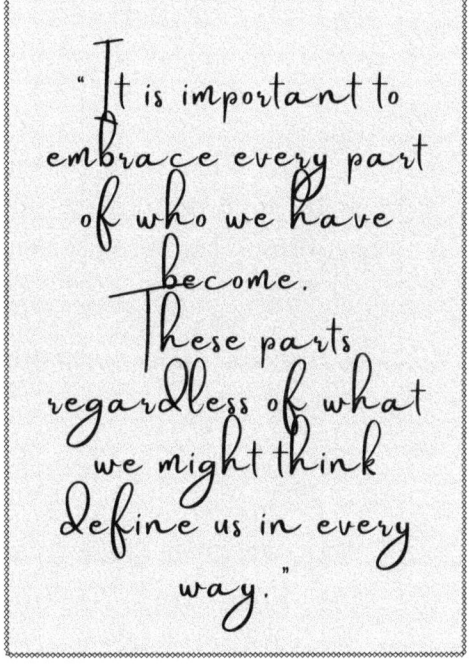

"It is important to embrace every part of who we have become. These parts regardless of what we might think define us in every way."

If we are able to sit, if only for a moment, with a sensation we would have previously labeled as *pain*, then we can expand the mind past our conscious patterning and ask, "What if? What if that is not pain? What if that were a sensation I could label as sensation?"

Can I now explore my body from a totally different lens?"

Translating that experience into daily life looks like re-imagining labels as questions—exploring the world around us as if for the first time without the construct that had been given and accepted as truth.

If we can move through the world with a questioning mind, expanding our consciousness then there becomes no grasping, no aversion. Our world is left with is.

SMALL FISH, BIG POND

One day, that concept stood confronting me bearing the marks of a robed Abbot Buddhist Monk

One of my biggest internal struggles was coming to terms with my own lack of meditation certification to prove to the world my worth, written on paper with pen.

Yes, I have thirty-plus years of practice in many meditation and mindfulness traditions and profound self awareness of personal trauma and PTSD.

But, and there it is—the word the negates all else before: *BUT*.

But, when a Buddhist Monk who was supposes to be my friend and mentor heard I was moving *Inner Warrior Spirit* to a retreat center in a small town in northern Washington, he said, " You are a small fish in a desert."

The first thing I wanted to do was wear that certification like a cloak, concealing myself from the world.

Only I have no certification. So his comment left me naked, exposed, afraid, and grasping for even air to breath, because my practice and helping others to their own healing has become my purpose in life.

So when that robed Abbot Buddhist Monk told me I was a small fish... A part of me died in that very moment.

* * *

"If you always start from a place of standing, you will never get to a place of understanding."

Clifford L. Carter

SOMATIC AWARENESS

NEUTRALIZING DIS-EASE COURSE MATERIAL

(8)

BRAIN SCIENCE

UNDERSTANDING THE BRAIN AND HOW we process information is key to proper *Somatic Awareness* mindfulness practice.

In meditation, there are six senses: seeing, tasting, touching, smelling, hearing, and *the Thinking Mind*.

We call the sixth sense *the Thinking Mind* because it accepts the information brought in from the other five senses. *The Thinking Mind* processes information and sends it to what I call *the mind space*.

The mind space is where all past experience has been stored. It is as if *the Thinking Mind* accesses a library with stores of information to then further process seeing, tasting, touching, smelling, and hearing.

Thinking—generated by intrusive thought or random thinking without input from our other five senses.

We process information in that way.

Sensation—Thought—Action

We first have an experience (*Sensation*) with one of our six senses. Then, the information travels to our *Thinking Mind*. From there, *the Thinking Mind* checks in with the mind space for reference (*Thought*).

If the stimulus has a connection to a past experience, we might have some idea how to proceed.

Next comes *Action*. Once we decide how to qualify the experience, we act upon those assumptions. If, for instance, we hear fireworks at a fourth of July celebration and immediately recount a dramatic past experience involving guns and a shooting incident. That might cause one to duck, fall to the ground, or even run away.

In the same way, we smell a fresh peach at farmer's market that may take us to the time our grandmother made peach pie and pulled it fresh out of the oven.

Somatic Awareness teaches us to experience sensations from a place of equanimity. The peach pie might have the same charge as the fireworks, even though we differently label experiences and are initially called to say one is good and one is bad.

When working with sensations, we first avoid the words *good* and *bad*, *pleasure* and *pain*. The reason is, we all have an idea what those feelings are, all too well.

Somatic Awareness expands our consciousness by accepting all phenomena as equanimous (calm and composed) or equal. Over time, that dissolves the grasping or aversion associated with any given sensation.

Sensation–Thought–Action is the processing of information.

Somatic Awareness adds two very important steps which enables us to view sensation with equanimity (mental calmness)—two additional steps to brain processing which enables one to expand our consciousness past old patterns and give rise to a more curious questioning mind. Acceptance—Letting go.

As sensations arise, followed by a thought, the action becomes *acceptance*. When we accept any situation, the body naturally releases, or lets go of, tension it might be holding on to, associated with a thought.

Sensation—Thought—Action—Acceptance—Letting go.

Somatic Awareness meditation practice is based on the structure of mind processing, followed by accepting and letting go. As we continue that process using first external sensations and then internal sensation, we re-pattern our nervous system in a way that external stimuli no longer triggers good or bad. It is simply a question.

Once we begin to replace pleasure and pain with the concept of all phenomena as sensation, exploring outside and inside our body, we begin to accept and let go.

"Consciousness. The state of being awake and aware of one's self and one's surroundings."

The purpose of sitting on a cushion on the floor is to generate a small amount of dis-ease. That helps us to begin to understand the difference between sensation/pleasure, and sensation/pain.

Once that understanding is stable, it becomes possible to relate that to the world around us in a much broader way.

Remember the fireworks and the peach pie?

The energy of the fireworks might be 'a pushing away' and the peach pie becomes 'a pulling toward'. The stimuli are less important than the will to pull and the will to push. In that place we focus our attention. The wanting and not wanting when the fireworks or the peach pie arise from sensation, we then become curious, which enables one to sit or stay with that experience for a moment longer. That's how we sit with our uncomfortableness or conversely our comfortableness—free from grasping or aversion.

Somatic Awareness teaches us to view the world from a place of curiosity—open accepting and letting go of past patterns which trigger us and later lead to pain and suffering.

STILL SHIT HAPPENS

> Lying awake, counting the seconds between the cars going by my bedroom window. I'm still awake and then it's minutes along, with tossing and turning, so the counting seemed like a nightly ritual.
>
> I recall the events of the day, trying to make sense of how, after so long and so much work, trauma still creeps into my life in the most unexpected ways.
>
> Even meeting with a veteran writing group. Yes, a new group and new people, so it's understandable. But I'd come so far. My old-informed self

planned the day for the new-wiser self and took note of the impending traffic and other possible obstacles.

I left my home about an hour early with thoughts of the road and each mile marker along the way. I'd driven that distance many times before, but this time was different. It had an outcome that could not be determined by the forthcoming events. I felt the anxiety in my body playing out by every stop and start, every turn and every time someone moved in and out of my lane. I did, however, notice my stomach rumbled and decided to stop at *Subway*.

When the light turned green, I squealed my tires to get through the light, only to immediately turn into the tiny parking lot.

The person inside behind the counter was nice enough, I guess, but like a robot of efficiency with words keyed into her hard drive, she said nothing more than what was necessary. That did not help my situation to push me past old self.

Back in my car, I decided to eat while driving—because still forty-five minutes early was not early enough. When taking a bite, I looked in my rearview mirror and noticed a young man behind me, inches from my bumper. The next time I stopped, I looked again as he lit a crack pipe.

I then imagined the scenario of being rear ended by an eighteen-year-old meth head with no insurance, actively smoking crack—he totals my car. I'm late for my writing class with forty-five minutes to spare. All that preparation...

You'd think that would be the reason I always leave early—to avoid life challenges. But that day, that was only the beginning.

I got to the library, after passing the entrance twice and pulled into a parking spot that seemed safe enough. Finishing my chips and drink, I cased the lot. Far too many people walking around, hanging out, and signs saying it was 'free to park' and other signs saying you have to 'pay to park'— incredibly confusing what to focus upon.

Looking around, I found a machine that seemed familiar and made my way over to it. Standing there looking at it for a minute or two asking myself, "Is it free? Is it pay? How does it know my car is here? Shit! There must be cameras everywhere."

Breathe. Don't panic, but there is a line forming behind me. Just do something.

I gathered my things and got to the front door of the library, took a deep breath, and went in. I asked the information lady where the veteran writing group was meeting.

She said, "Second floor, to the right."

Still half an hour early, I cased the joint and tried to relax before anyone got there. As I made my way up the winding stairway and crested the top, I was met with a seemingly sea of people sitting at tables and milling about—anxiety arose. I felt my heart race and I got dizzy. I could not breathe.

I remember seeing the ceiling while holding on to the handrail and turning myself around right there. I headed back down the stairs. Those first few steps were challenging. I'm not sure how I managed them except for just coming up and the memory still in my feet and legs of the spacing.

I saw myself falling, end over end, down to the bottom—and the people rushing over to help.

That idea in my mind clinched my hand around the railing so tightly, when I did finally reach the bottom, it was hard to let go.

I went into a room where I could be alone and started deep breathing and recounted what had happened. Feeling sensations in my body, accepting that was sensation and only that. Letting go of the experience that brought me to the very place and time, encapsulated by trauma.

Breathing, feeling sensations, being with sensation, and moving on. The practice I knew so well and still got blindsided by life. But don't we all?

I made it back up those stairs, focusing on my breath, feeling sensations. The cold handrail under my hand sensation. The steps under my feet sensation. The sounds of a library sensation.

Yes, I was five minutes late after all that planning and the early departure... but still, shit happens.

* * *

THE PROCESS:

BEGINNING WITH SENSATION, ENDING WITH LETTING GO.

All things in our life occur in that way. The energy we give to a thing lives in the process between *Thought* and *Action*. Only if we can be in *Acceptance* can we *Let Go*.

Dis-Ease is the feeling that lives in the space between *Sensation* and *Letting Go*. The breath, when focused upon, is the vehicle which carries you through difficult times.

"Sadness comes and sadness goes. Realize there was a time without sadness. Understand everything changes. Even sadness."

Clifford L. Carter

Somatic Awareness
Neutralizing Dis-Ease Course Material

(9)

Clinging & Craving

"It takes a village to heal our wounds."

Holding on to a thing or concept with a tight fist—meaning, the way we perceive the world and how we would like others to perceive us is correct, justified, or simply put, right.

That idea was generated by a grasping or aversion that then became solidified over time by being validated day after day, week after week, year after year.

That solid idea created a narrative by which we live our wants, needs, dreams by connecting only to the relationships that further attached us to the base.

Grasping and aversion is the pulling toward or the pushing away that over time can generate a clinging or need for the very thing we grasp. The same energy from aversion can create clinging and craving.

That's why clinging and craving are essentially the same attachment to something we might want really bad or something we have that we do not want, and we therefore attempt to hold that thought, concept, or even a tangible item from our past.

The craving and clinging comes from the need to be right. The need deepens as we come in contact with those who validate and those who challenge a particular concept. We dig in by justifying, word-smithing, sometimes bulling our way to rightness.

It's only when we understand rightness and wrongness are only concepts fueled by the need to feel safe at its core.

The notion of feeling safe is something we all like to feel, without exception. The question becomes, "Is it necessary to be right to feel that safety?"

In trauma, safety has been taken away and replaced with fear. When that happens, the tendency is to cling on to the patterns we believe to be true. That's a natural reaction, because patterning equals familiar, and familiar generates a feeling of peace and safety. It's like the routine of waking up in the morning at the same time, without much thought. A routine may begin by brewing a nice cup of coffee as we scroll through the day's news.

That routine, when disrupted, can cause a feeling that our day is somehow *off*. That may seem silly and illogical, but routine creates safety and ease and is something that becomes a mindless act until it is disrupted by any outside influence.

Somatic Awareness would ask us to disrupt or create a very small amount of dis-ease, to then challenge the solidity of any concept that has a clinging nature. By doing that, first using sensation in a way that we accept what is happening in the moment, we are able to dissect the concept.

Or, as I like to say. "Look at it from all sides of the tree."

When we can examine a sensation happening first outside the body, and as we go deeper inside the body, we connect with our true nature—free from patterns and the need to be right, generating the deeper need to feel safe. When exploring sensations from a questioning mind free from attachment, we begin to have a curiosity about the world we've created and imagine the tethers lifting by experiencing a different view.

When we cultivate questioning trauma triggers generated by a sensation, then qualified by the thinking mind, sensation becomes a curious exploration rather than a solidified knowing, followed by the same reaction, time and time again.

Somatic Awareness disrupts patterns and neutralizes clinging and craving by giving space to a questioning curiosity.

Below is a short essay of how habitual behavior becomes ritual. As a behavior becomes ritual, there is little mindfulness entering the circumstance in witch we are engaging.

MINDFULNESS AND RITUAL

> Mindfulness and ritual on the surface have similar characteristics—should not be confused or used together in general terms.
>
> Mindfulness is simply becoming aware of one's actions in any given moment in time to add focus

or attention so to see clearer the act in which one is involved.

Mindful breathing is simply focusing attention on the breath to become aware of what arises when focus or attention is placed there. Mindfulness can be used for any action or sensation you undertake or of which you want to become aware.

Ritual is born out of trauma—the need to control something out of our realm of controlling. When trauma occurs, we want to get away from it and one way to do that is by developing an activity that brings our mind to a mindless state.

Over and over, when we engage in a mindless state a habit forms. Every time a trigger sets off and takes us back to a traumatic event, we choose habitual activity to engage ourselves in mindlessness.

Over time, that can become ritualistic. When a trigger happens, a doorway starts to open and the mindless action that lead to the ritual forms in a way we do not even understand or are even conscious of.

Again, that is a mindless state brought on by trauma perpetuated by years or habit that become ritualistic.

Ritual is a very deep need to control our surroundings in every way. Step by step, material by material, person by person, in every way you can imagine.

The way out of mindless ritualistic habituation is *mindfulness*. Going about it first with slowing down the mind through meditation and mindfully entering the acts.

When a trigger occurs, the mind speeds up and clings to habit. Habituation leads to ritual. Once we are in ritual, we are essentially disassociated to the outside world.

There is no great difference between ritual and disassociation/disregulation. Both are an extreme need to *check out* of the world as triggers happen in any moment in time.

* * *

"Present actions are the consequences of past experiences."

Clifford L. Carter

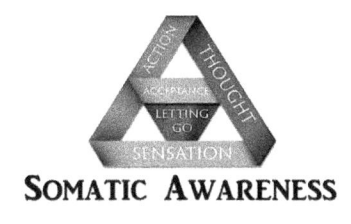

SOMATIC AWARENESS

NEUTRALIZING DIS-EASE COURSE MATERIAL

(10)

DEPENDENT ORIGINATION

THE IDEA ALL THINGS ORIGINATE from a source is *Dependent Origination.* That source, however distant in our past, informs and solidifies our present and future.

If we track an experience backwards, we find the source that influences our view of the present. It is that very idea that allows us to recognize all phenomena has a root or link to the past.

Somatic Awareness enables us to connect with self through sensations to not only recognize but explore and accept a sensation happening in the moment.

On the surface we might ask, "What does sensations have to do with past experience?"

As we have explored the *Somatic Awareness'* curriculum, *Neutralizing Dis=Ease,* we remember how human processing starts with sensation followed by thought and action.

Once we become aware of that process, we recognize the subtlety of sensations working inside our body, as well as sensations outside the body.

The nature of past experience starts with sensation stored in the body (or somatically understood in the mind) and held on to as truth.

If all phenomena passes through sensation, sensation must be the way out of the grasping and aversion that ultimately led to pain and suffering.

It is easy to recall being bitten by a small dog with puppies because of a scar still present on my leg. It is less about the memory than the idea that small dogs with puppies might not be so friendly—or holding on to fear that all dogs with puppies, or even all dogs, are not friendly.

It's hard to imagine that before approaching the small dog with puppies as an eight-year-old, the very experience was dependent on yet something that happened even before that. Maybe being bitten by a mother with puppies was a test or an expectation that the very thing would happen.

The solidifying of present day informs the future, influenced by the past.

The remedy becomes working deeper and deeper with our sensations, to be with, accept, and move on to the next sensation arising. That enables us to neutralize the effect of any past experience influencing our present by grasping or averting.

By neutralizing grasping and aversion, we can begin to see the world from a place of questioning and exploration without preconceived notions of how things are or are not.

Knowing right, wrong, good, and bad leads us to pain and suffering. A closed or narrow consciousness diminishes our true nature (or self) and shrouds that by solid, fixed ways we see ourselves, our surroundings, and how we want others close to us to see and experience our world through an ego-driven lens.

Somatic Awareness—intentionally working with outside sensations—teaches us how our brain processes information. As we work with sensations happening inside the body, we begin to notice connections to our outside world. Those connections, when we use the process of being with, accept, and moving on to the next sensation arising allows us to explore sensations, find connection, and ultimately let go of the dependency on our past patterns, as well as the sources of those past patterns.

> "Planting seeds with the right sunlight, right water, right nurture will later bear shade and fruit for generations to come."

In Buddhism, that process is depicted as links of a chain, connecting all clinging to past sensation.

In western psychology, past experience lives in the mind and thus can be processed through cognitive processing—or thinking our way through a unpleasant situation by simply exploring the past, recognizing it is not happening today thus it loses its power by processing through our brain.

That can be useful when working with a triggering experience, but realizing a current event has been influenced by our past allows us to cut off and break the link to the current, thus impeding future recurring.

Cutting the link that facilitated the energy that, in turn, created the trigger, dismantles the attachment to a future need to validate our belief system.

Somatic Awareness, by working deeply with sensations, cuts the cause that affects us in the present time.

THE MIND/THINKING MIND PARADIGM.

We can think of *the Mind* as a container—a place from where action is born. A place to store all past experience, enabling a holding on to an idea in the present, informed by the past, that has the capacity to cling. Left alone, *the Mind* itself is a neutral space—settling like a calm pool of water below a breathless afternoon sky.

Sensations entering *the Thinking Mind* processed by *the mind space* begin to take hold of today's experience from a time far gone. Holding forms attachments to an outcome that describes our present self and binds us to the very way we experienced the world. Without past reference, the mind-body experience becomes neutral.

Neutral shares not grasping and no aversion to a thing, only curiosity. Questioning mind expands our consciousness and allows space to view the world from a lens of endless possibilities—awe and wonder, child mind, or as I call it "green sky"—a new paradigm opening a portal to begin to see clearly from your own true nature, free from the patterns that bind us.

The Thinking Mind is only another sense, in addition to the five senses not mentioned in our childhood classroom. *The Thinking Mind* is always active. The only time we notice we are not thinking is when our awareness has moved to another sensation, like seeing, tasting, touching, smelling, or hearing. At that very moment we begin thinking.

Awareness moves from place to place to place. The need to input information in *the Mind*, that container waiting to be filled with present experience—only to find connection with the past, grasping to feel safe in the moment's sensation, and dream for the future.

If familiar experience were neither good nor bad, would there be a need to grasp or avert?

Would we be able to be with sensation, enter into sensation, and really see, taste, touch, smell, hear, and think about a sensation?

It is challenging as an adult who has experienced many things in life to see grey, middle, or a sense of wonder.

If we could look deeply into sensation—so deeply we are no more *knowing*, only exploring. So deeply you are mindful of every curve, temperature change, thickness, or thinness in the present sensation.

Focus on the breath, become aware of sensation, be with sensation, accept sensation, and move on to the next sensation arising. Place that experience in *the Mind* and notice if it becomes neutral. See if the experience has been transformed in any way.

When transformation happens, our mind expands by the very need to store new information. That mixes with past experiences and challenges our belief system.

That challenge creates space for a new paradigm—a way to be in the world free from the tethers to our past.

Any obsessive act is a consequence born out of pain and suffering, usually caused by trauma. The way to end that is to first accept the behavior, instead of seeing it as *bad* and pushing the behavior away.

Then and only then is one able to more clearly see behind the behavior. Find the root cause, then again accept the root cause, see it more clearly, and one will (at some point) be able to let go of the behavior by letting go of its original dependency.

"It's all around us...
All the answers
to all our questions are
no further away
than our six senses."

Clifford L Carter

SOMATIC AWARENESS
NEUTRALIZING DIS-EASE COURSE MATERIAL

(II)

QUESTIONING MIND

THE IDEA WE DO NOT know a thing after years of education, wisdom, and simply being in the world can be a hit to the ego.

Well, that's the point.

What if we knew nothing at all, beginning from a place of curiosity? Like transforming oneself to another plane of existence where our surroundings, language, colors, shapes, etc., cannot be explained as familiar. How does that impact our existence on this so-called plane? Does it give rise to fear, acceptance, curiosity, or simply exploration with a searching for some reference to our past?

For a moment, consider a child born into a life that is full of wonder, awe, and the need to explore. Given the guidance and safety of an adult who previously navigated that environment with experience of right, wrong, good, bad, pleasure and pain. For a time, the child is able to formulate their own interpretation of color, shapes, feelings as to their surroundings—viewing the world from a place of awe and wonder, curious exploration.

The Mind expands with ideas of our surroundings without the need to qualify as good, bad, safe or unsafe. As the child grows with more and more information about their new world, an adult might enter the space, qualifying and naming, solidifying the ideas and patterns born out of awe and wonder without the need to question and explore. *The Mind* starts to catalog that information for future reference.

> "We are all interconnected to each other and every living thing. Where there is pain or pleasure, there is wisdom and understanding of self. We must be open to the lessons in both for true transformation to occur."

When the object or experience returns, the child feels confident in *knowing*. As the child interacts with other children who have had similar experiences—as long as a reference holds true—their bonds become strong, creating attachment.

If the reference to any given view is seen as opposite, the bond is weakened. Without validation of qualifying and knowing an experience, an aversion to the other starts to form. That validation of experience becomes the start of solidifying one's mind. Seeing the world through a certain lens not truly our own, but a construct from our own past experience, is informed by the very adult who influenced it.

Is that our experience or simply the ideas of another? And if true, then the other's experience was formed in much the same way—from generations to generations, past leading to the future.

Can we, as adults, become curious again by accepting our sensations, letting go of the attachment of right and wrong, good or bad?

The start of that process is questioning our every interaction with the world around us, much like we did as a child—without knowing or influenced by another. Walking through the world, questioning without labeling good, bad, safe, unsafe. The sounds we believe we know, stepping back into a place of not knowing. A place of what is unknown about a sound, letting go of what we do know.

Understanding what we do know has been handed down from generation after generation.

EXPANDED MIND

> One night, I heard a sound coming from my garage. My first thought was a squirrel had gotten in, looking for food and could not manage to get out before I closed the door.
>
> When I opened the door, that squirrel jumped from a ledge a few feet from my head, scaring the daylights out of me. Looking around for said squirrel, I came across a curious little animal that was

not a squirrel, at all. I had no idea of what it could be and was mesmerized by its eyes looking at me—looking at it from behind stored pillows.

It seemed to be friendly and certainly as curious of me as I was of it. As I watched the little animal move around the garage, I noticed a big furry tail with rings. I thought, *Raccoon*, but it did not fit the brief of a large dark body, mask-faced creature I knew from my childhood.

The little creature was long and sleek, like a ferret I had seen at a local pet shop. Surely, that was someone's pet who had found its way into my garage. Its tail did not match a ferret, so what was that peeking at me, seemingly unafraid and curious?

As my mind expanded, due to a truly new experience, the feeling of joy became overwhelming. The idea I had no idea what that creature was—and there it was, looking at me looking at it.

* * *

Clifford L. Carter

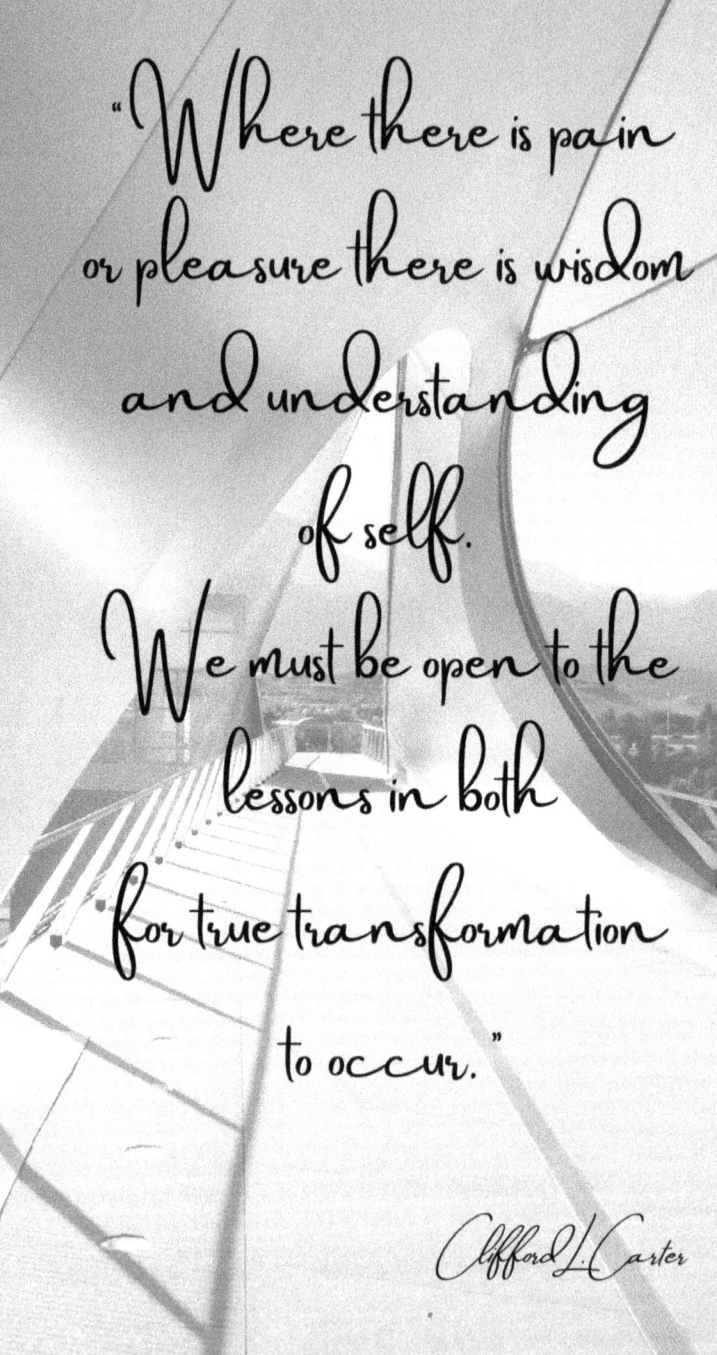

"Where there is pain or pleasure there is wisdom and understanding of self. We must be open to the lessons in both for true transformation to occur."

Clifford L. Carter

Somatic Awareness
Neutralizing Dis-Ease Course Material

(12)

Radical Acceptance

WHAT IS RADICAL ACCEPTANCE?

SEEING EACH OF US AS humans first and understanding we are on our own paths to a greater realization of our purpose.

Looking inside ourselves and seeing our true nature and believing we have the capacity to feel all emotions ever felt by our fellow human beings.

Looking outside ourselves and seeing others as we see ourselves.

Accepting my path leads me to the same destination as everyone else.

Accepting there are many correct paths and many places on the path at one time on many paths to one destination.

Accepting I do not have all the answers to all the questions.

Accepting change is a constant. Good and bad is an idea formulated in the mind to enable us to feel safe in our world.

Labeling is the opposite of letting go and accepting there is another alternative.

Letting go leads to *Radical Acceptance.*

The state of being in the world that does not grasp for known meaning as it was given, yet is open to possibility. Clinging is to fear *the known that was taught/ given* would somehow be challenged by accepting another alternative.

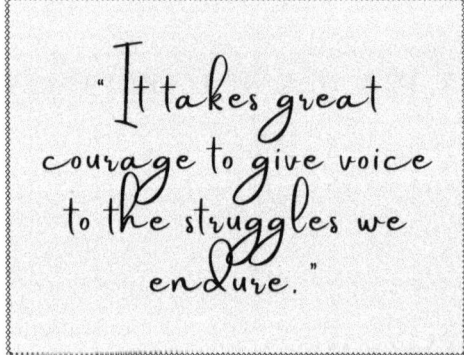

When we radically accept ourselves with all our ideas, we can become open to seeing the world from a less-bound existence. Self acceptance becomes the key to radical acceptance and freedom to experience the world from a place of wonder—a place of question—and begin to realize the interdependency of all living beings, both plants and animals, natural and unnatural.

WHAT IS EFFORTLESS CHANGE?

Transforming in a way that does not hold both grasping nor aversion. Movement through accepting and letting go.

Does change stem from an inner idea something is misplaced in the beginning?

It seem to me that acceptance followed by letting go facilitates the unencumbered inner effortless change required to transform oneself.

Karma is like that...

At some point Karma will ripen like an apple ready to eat. When it's ripe, the cause will decide the sweetness or bitter taste.

Life is a series of holding on to and letting go of. In the simplest way, we hold on to the things that connect us to our past in the hope of solidifying our future. It is the holding on to that tethers us to pain, suffering, joy, and happiness.

That holding also disables us from being in discovery each and every moment. It is in the space of discovery that the doorway to letting go of past inabilities, discouragements, shoulds and shouldn'ts, becomes available.

When we live in the present moment, we not only embrace the *now,* but we also plant and cultivate seeds for a future free from suffering—free from the 'who we have been' and embrace the 'who we may truly become' and were always meant to be.

Being is not about movement which way. It is not about action. It is about being *okay*.

Being *okay* in a situation without the need to change or alter the outcome for self or any other participants.

As long as we do not choose, everything remains the same. The moment the decision of good-bad, right-wrong, happy-sad is made, our possibilities no longer exist.

Accepting a thing opens one to explore without judgment. Judgment is based on the past, solidified by clinging. Acceptance allows one to let go. When we can accept, all phenomena move freely through us unencumbered by attachment.

As a society we are programmed to try. If only we try, we can do anything. The path to awakening is first acceptance followed by letting go. There is no *trying* in accepting or letting go, simply being, allowing and awakening.

Transformation is also the process of first accepting and then letting go. We all share the same capacity to transform. The process may not always look or feel a way we might like, but when we become open to the experience, our lives will imagine true change.

"HOME IS WHERE THE HEART IS."

The true home is where one's affections are centered.

If that is true, then what if our affections have always been centered in hostile or an unwelcome place?

The obvious answer is to move one's affections. Is it really that simple? Like packing a *U-haul*, driving off into the sunset, or finding a warm feathered nest to lay your head for awhile until the pulling and tugging brings us back home?

What if the heart's home were centered inside? Without longing, a nest filled with feathers, or a place of past memory?

Sensation feeds the mind. The mind connects to past experience and generates clinging to what was, what could have been, and what might be.

Never what is.

We are all interconnected to each other and every living thing. Where there is pain or pleasure there is wisdom and understanding of self.

We must be open to the lessons in both for true transformation to occur. Life is not only one sided but multiple sides of the same paradigm, explaining the true meaning of our experiences. Gaining that knowledge will lead us to our final destination of understanding true self, true nature—the one true unchanging core that connects us all.

MY SAFE PLACE

I recently had a realization that left me questioning my presumptions about my personal safety. After fifty-four years of searching for a safe place to live, safe place to work, and safe place to just be, I came across the most unusual environment that would leave me wondering. Yet every time I went there, I fell into a state of calm.

Who in their right mind feels safe in prison? Well, I guess some of the inmates might. After questioning a few of them, I learned one of the reasons they find themselves back in prison is the world outside feels increasingly unsafe. That made sense to me, but in my case, I had never been to prison. Yet, the safety I felt behind bars was intriguing.

Wednesday morning, getting up before dawn cracks, I took a shower and was on the road before heavy traffic. I never beat the rush hour traffic, but I always save just enough time to stop at the 7-11 for a toilet break, a muffin, and a drink. I never figured out where the bathroom was inside the prison once the last steel door shut me inside, locking me and six to eighteen inmates together in a room.

Finding a parking spot at the prison was challenging, so I accepted the first one available in the far *North 40*. I emptied my pocket of any change or foreign objects. No cell phone or wallet, only the essential ID card, meditation cushion, and my Tibetan bells were allowed. Allowed only after approval by volunteer services. Signing in to the roster was next, with name, organization, date, time, reason for visit, and where I was going.

I turned my ID over to the guard and he replaced it with a non-escort badge and a push-button panic buzzer. My car keys went inside a locker along with anything else I forgot to leave in the car. I proceeded through the metal detector, holding my breath. Even though I had done that a dozen times before.

Once through the first gate (controlled by the tower) I breathed again and became more relaxed. Opened and closed behind me, and on to the next gate. Once inside, I approached the steel doors smashing into the solid steel embankments.

No one is coming in or out unless they have prior approval.

The first one unlocked like a giant steel safe, slid open on an un-oiled yoke and slammed into a socket tight enough to hold water, and closed behind me before the next one opened.

This is what safety looks like, sounds like, feels like.

Walking across the green to the therapeutic community, I witnessed hundreds of inmates, some training dogs, others raking gravel, and most just making their way from one side of the campus to the other, like me.

Once inside, I again found my classroom and placed yoga blocks in a circle formation. Yoga blocks instead of meditation cushions because they are easier to clean. Also, the ladies are less likely to conceal a shank in a yoga block.

That was when it got interesting.

The ladies filed in and sat down, cross-legged. Focused on the breath, became aware of sensations inside and outside their bodies, stood and walked in meditation, again focusing on their breath and became aware they were walking.

* * *

Confidentiality keeps me from sharing what was spoken in my groups and why that had become my safe space. I can say those ladies were real and they were raw.

Real in the sense they had nothing to lose—they've already lost it all and were starting over. Sometimes not for the first or second time.

I found kinship with those ladies in that my life had been about a series of starting over, again and again. I found a place where people have no reason to hide who they are, from where they've come, and where they dream of going.

I was fortunate enough to share myself—real and raw—with no reason to hide who I am, where I'm going, and my dreams for the future.

They filed out of class the same way they came in. I'm not sure who saved whom. I only hope we at least had an even exchange of hope and challenge.

"Childhood trauma stems the roots of great pain for generations if not properly weeded."

Clifford L. Carter

Somatic Awareness
Neutralizing Dis-Ease Course Material

(13)

Seeing and Seeing Deeply

PAWPAW

Sometimes it's difficult to return to a place of my childhood—to that place of awe and wonder so full of imagination.

My father was a hunter in every sense of the word.

What that means to me is every sensation I experienced in the world was through the countryside of southern Illinois.

As the frost met the rise of the sun on a fall morning, it formed a haze through the low-lying woodland bottom. The sound of acorns cracked from treetops while we walked along a worn deer trail.

Squirrel season was one of my dad's favorite times of year. I was often by his side with my .410

shotgun, hunting vest—fast asleep in the truck or next to a solid oak tree.

I remember one trip in particular because it was one of my favorite places. My cousins lived on a farm outside Hardin, Illinois. Hardin was known for apples, peaches, pears, and pumpkins. The fall was apple and pumpkin season, along with squirrel and another season I had yet to have any idea about.

Waking up so early to the pushing and pulling of my little shoulder and the sound of my father's voice.

"Get up. We need to go."

I rolled out of bed and, of course, made it up as fast as I could before I ran downstairs to the box of hunting gear. Thermal underwear from top to bottom, thick socks pulled up to my knees made electric shocks on my legs, then I covered up everything with overalls and a heavy jacket.

Grabbing my .410 shotgun and a box of shells, I climbed in the old pickup where my dad was waiting—beagles loaded, engine running, heater on. Dad reached into a bag of tobacco for a pinch.

We always stopped at Forkeyville for gas. Dad loved to shoot the shit with the guys about hunting dogs, and that's likely the real reason he went to that station.

Most of the trip for me was spent fast asleep, while the truck rocked and rolled along country roads. I occasionally woke up to the smell of *Red Man* chewing tobacco spit onto the rusted-out floor of that old truck, running out onto the blacktop.

Red Man had a fresh smell when you opened the foil-lined paper sack. I quite liked it. But after it had been chewed around in one's check and gum for a time, the aroma (circling with spit) changed to a putrid sniff—as if it had been pickled for months in a fruit jar set out in the hot summer sun.

The drive to Calhoun County was about fifty miles and a woke up to the draw bridge just before you got to Hardin. Excitement was hardly containable for a boy anticipating the drawing of the bridge. If you were lucky enough (and I had been on occasion) to be the first car in line when the bridge raised, it was the best seat on the road. *Click, click, click* as the bridge went up and excitement mounted as the river barge effortlessly floated under.

> "Seeing the sky green is the beginning of forgetting everything we were taught and believed to be true."

Hardin was a river town with a couple restaurants, maybe one gas station, and meat market along the Mississippi that most likely will flood again this year as it does almost every year. Driving through, up and down, on the blacktop to the other side of town—we passed farms and orchard alike—the riverbed on our left and the Illinois hills to the right.

Then, the truck turned down a gravel road and through three creeks where my cousins lived and the best squirrel hunting, apple, peach, pumpkin picking and, if you are lucky enough, arrowheads.

That day, we pulled up and let the beagles out. He headed for the woods—squirrel would be the hunt and the game of the day on the mind of the hunter on that crisp fall day in Calhoun County, Illinois.

As we entered the woods, the sounds of the forest closed in around me as if I entered a sacred place. Bird sounds, nuts falling, and cracks from the frozen leaves under my feet signaled my entry to that magical place. I was silent and yet sound was all around me.

A beautiful red fox made its way across a ridge in the distance, his fury tail so big it was like a giant bottle brush red and brown in color.

My dad spotted something in the distance I had never seen before and have never seen again in all my life. It was a small tree, not much taller than him. It had giant leaves and an oval-shaped yellowish fruit hanging from its branches. The smell was much like banana, as was the texture when Dad picked one, pulled his *Barlow* knife, sliced it opened, and handed me one half to try.

First my tongue, then my teeth took a bite, chewing—or more like smashing between my teeth and swallowing.

"What is this?" I asked. I had never seen, or tasted such a thing before. And to come across something like that in the hills of Illinois that appeared to be a tropical fruit was certainly magical.

Dad said it was a Pawpaw. They grew in many places in Illinois, but it was unusual to find a small tree with so much fruit on it as that one, and at just the right time. They were ripe.

"Their season doesn't last long," he went on to say, "It's our lucky day to be able to find a Pawpaw tree in the middle of our squirrel hunt."

That day I'm not sure if we came home with even one squirrel ready for mother to fry up with mashed potatoes and white gravy and squirrel giblets, or even if a beagle made a sound all morning in those woods with acorns cracking and falling to the ground.

I do know I found a Pawpaw tree. From that moment on, squirrel hunting with my dad included a taste of something magical—an experience I had never had before and would never have again. I saw a red fox with a tail as big as a giant bottle brush, and smelled fermented chewing tobacco while watching a barge float down the river, pushing coal under a draw bridge in Hardin, Illinois, and eating freshly picked apples from my cousin's orchard.

* * *

Most of us move through our world observing our surroundings from a lens, viewed through our past experience. Only noticing the surface, then deciding what we are seeing in context of a life-long past—a practical reason for seeing that has no space or time for seeing deeply.

Seeing and evaluating the world around us, like rapid fire, enables us to qualify our surroundings. That qualifying is an attempt to know if we are safe or unsafe. The need to evaluate and come to some conclusion, either good or bad, brings about a feeling of ease. Even in the instance of an unsafe feeling, the ease that arises is that we know the experience. The knowing generates ease. The simple knowing how to approach the situation creates a rightness thus generates a level of comfort.

There is another possibility while observing our environment. It lands somewhere between safe and unsafe. I define that space as neutral. Like a car that is neither going forward nor in reverse, it is the gear that is static. Waiting, if on level surface, or very slowly rolling forward or backward depending on the terrain.

As we recognize and qualify our environment, we, too, move forward, backward, or sit in neutral for a moment—searching our mind for some sort of reference that is either drawing or reeling.

Seeing deeply becomes engaged when we sit in neutral, exploring the what-we-do-not-know about our surroundings.

What if we approached the world from a place of not knowing?

It might sound a little scary to be dropped in a space of confusion without any reference. I would encourage another approach of seeing the world that includes seeing deeply or looking close enough to see what-we-do-not-know or understand. In that space of wonder our mind and consciousness open to many possibilities.

It's easy to become stuck on a concept that is not our own but are born in to, believed to be true, and further validated by our actions. Challenging those views can be overwhelming but also very freeing in that our beliefs have a tendency to bind us to circumstance.

When talking about trauma as it relates to patterning, we become prisoners to our own experience by defining what is about to happen with a cloudy lens—a lens that has been smudged by a traumatic event or a number of events. The seeing becomes more and more narrow as we attempt to move away and quickly return to the same outcome over and over again.

Mindfulness, when combined with the focusing on the breath, gives space and a more clear calm so we might have just a moment to see deeply. Imagine what we do not know, what is on the edges of the cloudy lens that has been darkened by the very trauma itself.

As a sensation arises, informing us, labeling our experience, by taking time to focus on our breath and simply becoming aware of sensations, we can begin to give space between safe or unsafe. In that neutral space, we get the chance to explore seeing deeply. Setting aside judgments, returning to the breath, and further deepening our experience to what we do not know.

Again, that not knowing has the capacity to reinterpret the outcome in a way that does not further our fixed ideals. Thus, putting one's mind to ease and neutralizing components of a traumatic event that one day has little power over our present experience.

Seeing deeply, exploring the unknown or neutral parts is a way of separating the fabric of our consciousness to allow greater understanding, acceptance and letting go.

"The new you will always have fragments of the old you, however small. Be with, accept, and move on to wherever and however they continue to arise."

Clifford L. Carter

SOMATIC AWARENESS

NEUTRALIZING DIS-EASE COURSE MATERIAL

(14)

DIS-EASE

The idea that disease and dis-ease are similar and different at the very same time holds true in that they are both maladies. One of the mind and the other, the body. Although there can be disease of the brain that would be different than the dis-ease of the mind.

When moving through the world, all things or phenomena come and go with or without attachment. If there was a past experience with phenomena, then attachment to the definition or the rightness or wrongness began to take hold. From the holding creates clinging and craving. Not for the defining, but the idea the defining is necessary or we cannot be the 'who we believe ourselves to be'. It is the holding or clinging on to the rightness as if it was life dependent.

The idea that rightness can be so attached to self comes from the need to feel safe. That need to feel safe comes from the idea the world around us is inherently unsafe, thus motivating one to search for safety by means of identifying and living only in a space of knowing. That way further becomes solid by operating from the lens or idea that I must know therefore I am safe.

As a child, there was little knowing, and one would think the world must be unsafe from a child's point of view. We attempt to provide a safe environment for the child to explore, question, and even make a few mistakes under the supervision of an adult.

> "Grasping outside ourself in an attempt to manage internal struggle seems backward but I guess its human nature when we think we are not enough."

As the child grows both in stature and mind, they are filled with rights and wrongs, safes and unsafes. These are not of the child but of the adult supervision of the child's thoughts, words, and actions. Further solidified by formal or informal education. As the concepts continually become reinforced, attachment takes hold.

That attachment is to the right and wrong. safe and unsafe, not to the phenomena present in the moment. The phenomena were simply catalysts viewed through the portal of sensation.

The way back to self unencumbered by attachment began with curiosity. Once we were open to an idea, we had an opportunity to freely explore. Without attachment, we are able to rewire any situation, viewing all aspects to find our own conclusion.

That is the beginning of accepting and letting go of past understanding influenced by those around us solidified by our own actions.

"Life is not one sided but multiple sides of the same paradigm explaining the true meaning of our experience."

Clifford L. Carter

SOMATIC AWARENESS

NEUTRALIZING DIS-EASE COURSE MATERIAL

(15)

REMEDY

PURPOSE COMES TO MIND WHEN thinking about how to transform one's self. The idea we are a part of something bigger than ourselves can motivate us to move through obstacles, far and wide. The purpose of self exploration is the ability to transform one's self. Imagine if we could see the world as color, shape, sound, etc., without naming and qualifying good, bad, pleasure, pain. How accessible would our world become if we could take off the guardrails that we learned and believed to be true?

True freedom is to exist without fear.

In the first days of the COVID-19 pandemic when we were confined to our homes, I imagined how challenging it would be focusing on myself, day in and day out. It was frightening to think not of how and when I would die from the flu, but how I would be forced to live with self. Avoiding self was my way of surviving the six-month-long COVID lockdown by creating purpose.

STITCHING WELLNESS

I remember thinking COVID would eventually go, along with each stress and trauma trigger I faced every waking moment of every day during the lockdown, unaware of the who, what, where, and how the flu might show itself. The beginning weeks had been particularly difficult for me as I struggled with isolation and abandonment in a way that might seem counterintuitive to most.

As a US Navy Submarine Veteran, a PTSD survivor, and the founder of the non-profit, Inner Warrior Spirit, my focus had been teaching mindfulness meditation as a way to counter trauma's effects.

"Where there is pain or pleasure there is wisdom waiting to be found."

In the beginning of the pandemic, my focus had still been on mindfulness meditation to keep me centered through the ups and downs. As I felt myself falling deeper and deeper into depression, using my mindfulness practice, looking inward, I realized what I needed in my life was purpose.

Something bigger than me. Something I could control when nothing else in my life felt controllable.

That night, April 2nd, 2020 I designed a face mask. The first go around was not great but not bad either. April 3rd, I built a box, dug a hole and, with the help of my neighbor who painted the box, we installed that box in my front yard. I placed sign on the box: FREE MASKS.

I took pictures, posted on *Facebook,* and started cutting and sewing face masks. Filling the box day after day and even shipping masks to North Carolina, West Virginia, California, and Denver, alike. Focusing on the breath and being aware I was cutting, sewing, stringing, bagging, and shipping.

The breath I could let go of. The cutting, the sewing, the bagging, the shipping, and giving, I could control and then let go.

What saved my life during the COVID-19 lockdown?

PURPOSE

* * *

My story seems filled with warm and fuzzy feelings of doing good in the face of unknown. The truth is, purpose can sometimes be the greatest avoidance strategy of all time. I easily justified being filled with *doing good for others* while remaining seemingly selfless.

The truth is my purpose had become selfish, as it was an attempt to survive in the face of loneliness with only myself to question.

The way back to self was a hard road, accepting and letting go of the tethers which held me to the very thoughts that brought about fear was challenging.

The remedy became clear when I understood any action that moves one away from self can be an avoidance strategy. There are, of course, actions we must accept as necessary for life as eating, sleeping, defecating. The rest are choices to check in with self or check out of self.

The remedy is checking in with self from the lens of questioning mind exploring what we know and do not know accepting and letting go.

CLIFFORD L. CARTER

"Right understanding leads to happiness."

Clifford L. Carter.

Somatic Awareness
Neutralizing Dis-Ease Course Material

(16)

Our Mind is Not Its Own

Growing up, my father shared how he had a severe drinking problem when he was in the Navy. So bad that in his own words, "I had to be strapped to a bed for two weeks to be dried out."

That was pretty scary to me when I first heard it, as I was about eight or nine years old and had never seen him drink. I didn't know him to attend any AA meetings, counseling, or for that matter anything that would outwardly change the kind of behavior he spoke about.

As a child growing up, even before the story that my father shared with me, the other thing which became apparent to me was how my father was able to transfer alcoholism to other activities. He also was able to transfer anger from coworkers to activities and other helpless living creatures so never to raise his hand to me, and only once to my brother (when he was a teenager) that I can remember.

I became a 'coon hunter at a very early age. You might think that was somewhat normal for a country boy growing up in the Midwest, whose father made shotgun shells. I was carried on my dad's shoulders through the woods before I could walk.

Spending time with my father was important to him—hunting when hunting season was in and fishing the rest of the year. Sounds like an amazing childhood growing up hunting and fishing in the woods and on the Mississippi river. While viewing it from the outside, it would seem that way.

I realized the damage had been done not by the lifestyle growing up but by the way my father used hunting, fishing, and dogs to teach me lessons and the behaviors that would shape my life languages for years to come. Long after my realization of how my father transferred his alcohol abuse as a young adult to hunting, fishing, dogs, fighting, and all the other activity in which he compulsively engaged, was the compulsive behavior that enabled him to check out of self when triggered from his past.

> "Accepting self just as we are enables us to accept others just as they are."

Looking back at the memory of my father, I realized he was unable to manage suffering in a healthy way. His lifestyle became an extension of alcoholism.

I could clearly see his drinking transferred to smoking, then chewing, fishing, hunting, dog training and literally every activity in which my father engaged.

Much like I remember Grandpa rolling his own cigarettes with *Prince Albert* tobacco and chewing tobacco later contributed to Grandpa's diagnosis of gum cancer, followed by his death.

DAD'S STRATEGY

Dad spit in a *Styrofoam* cup with a wadded up paper towel in it (so if it tipped over it wouldn't leak out on the seat of the truck) when we were on our way to his favorite hunting spot. Sometimes he used an empty *Pepsi* or *Tab* soda can. Those were a little more risky, trying to remember it was not an ice cold can of my favorite soda rather a container of his spit and tobacco.

The best idea was a old Chevy truck with a hole in the floorboard next to the driver's side door, a few inches from his hunting boot. Dad spit on the floor and it dripped onto the pavement.

That was great for me because as we mostly did 'coon hunting on a school night, I slept on the way to the woods and the way home. Sometimes waking up in a fog, I never knew if we stopped and picked up a cold drink while I had been sleeping.

In those days, school for me was the woods and the river. I did, however, graduate with a high school diploma as it was a requirement for joining the US Navy Submarine service.

My dad worked rotating shifts at the local ammunition factory. Shifts for him looked like one week on days, next week on evenings, and the next week midnights. Rotating back to days for the following thirty-five years of my father's life until he retired at age sixty-five.

Most times when my father was not sleeping before or after a shift, he would have me in hunting clothes as soon as I got home from school.

Other times, he prepared trout lines by stringing a main line from tree to tree in the back yard, after attaching leaders with hooks every two feet. Most lines were fifty- to 100-hooks long. That gave plenty opportunities to catch a hungry catfish, carp, bass, or alligator gar fish swimming by.

He then carefully carved notches in the sides of a old wooden crate that held every hook in place until the trout line was dropped into the river and sank down to the bottom with a heavy steel window weight. The other end was securely tied to a tree branch, jutting out over the Mississippi.

Reading *Tri County 'Coon Hunter* magazine and talking very loudly on the black wall-mounted kitchen phone with a fifteen-foot twisty black cord, he shared stories with his hunting buddies. Most sentences included, "Bitch" (female dog), "I'll be Goddamn"... after listening to the tales his 'coon hunting buddies relayed.

My dad was in a car accident where he ran into a train before he joined the Navy or maybe shortly after. He lost much of the hearing in his right ear.

Good hearing in both ears is important when you are a 'coon hunter, so you can determine the direction your dog is barking. In 'coon hunting, the dog changes their bark from a ball mouth (long drawn-out sound) when they are tracking to a chop mouth (short sound, over and over) when the animals are treed.

Direction is important because a raccoon can travel a pretty long distance and in circles before he goes up a tree—across water, over logs, in and out of holes and all kinds of interesting places, attempting to escape the hounds. If you can't tell direction, you'll have trouble 'coon hunting.

My dad loved 'coon hunting. We always had Walkers, Blue Ticks, Red Bones, and my favorites Black and Tans.

'Coon hunting on its own is a hobby for most, except for someone escaping their own pain and suffering—like my dad. It was a way to avoid self when life became overwhelming. It was my dad's way of self medicating, his avoidance strategy. Blocking out the pain and suffering that arose from his daily struggles with self.

A walk in the woods, feeling the ground beneath the foot, looking up and counting stars while listening to the dogs and plotting out the direction they headed and ending the night by killing something.

We always had four-plus dogs. Mostly 'coon hound dogs and sometimes beagles for hunting rabbit. Yes, we did not just hunt raccoon. We hunted rabbit, squirrel, pheasant, quail, dove, deer—almost anything that moved, we hunted. Either for selling the fur or to fill my mother's stew pot.

My dad came home from work often enraged about the job or someone he was working with, while hanging on a poker face at the dinner table. He quietly shoveled down his fill of meat and potatoes.

I could tell he was about to explode at any moment, and sometimes he did, waving his hand in the air while threatening to cut a hickory switch from a tree in the back yard.

Instead, after he cleaned his plate, he made his way to the basement where the hunting clothes were cleaned and stored, ready for the next hunt. Ready for a night in the woods with the dogs, as I sat at the kitchen table trying to do my homework.

My dad called upstairs, saying, "Come on. Get down here. Get ready. Let's go. You know I need your ear. I can't tell the direction the dogs are without you."

"But the books...?"

"Put your hunting clothes on and let's go."

We loaded up the dogs in the back of the truck and were off to the first hunting sites, unless we were lucky enough to get one or two 'coons at the first place we released the dogs. As my dad drove down the road, I felt the bumps and turns and smelled the *Red Man* chewing tobacco.

I fell fast asleep on the way to our hunting journeys, each and every night, stopping along a dirt road likely meant for a farm tractor with giant tires, navigating the muddy edges of a corn field. Most of the places we hunted were too secluded for anyone to even know we were there unless we got too close to a farmhouse or we neglected to ask for permission to hunt, and then we would be met with the barrel of a shotgun.

Sometimes we heard a farmer shoot a gun, not knowing if it was in our direction or up in the air. Never-the-less, it was a sign we were not welcome. We called in the dogs and moved on to another spot. We turned the dogs out to see if they could pick up a track, while we fired up the carbide lights, and off we went.

Carbide, a chemical compound we used in a container, when combined with water let off a gas which held a flame. The container, flame, and mirror all attached to a helmet which sat atop one's head. It lit our way in the woods at night as well as a cigarette. It started a small camp fire in the winter months.

I remember shaking the carbide up and watching the flame get bigger and bigger.

The only thing that got in the way of a good 'coon hunt was deer. When the dogs jumped a deer and decided they wanted to have a go, the chase was on.

Moving quickly through the woods with a chop bark and the long pauses meant they lost the trail. Mostly running the deer by sight alone and most of the time so far away that when the dog realized they were out of range, it took hours for them to get back to us.

We walked fast and even ran through the woods to get to them.

Sometimes, we called for them and then gave up and went back to the truck. If they didn't come back (which was the best result), my dad placed his coat on the ground and took me home. It was, however, a school night, so I could go to bed. But, I would later discover the real reason I would be taken home and my dad would return to collect his dogs.

He always said when he went back, he found the dogs laying on his coat just where he had left it. That was not always the case for a couple reason. Sometimes he came back and the dogs weren't there.

Sometimes when we were out and the dogs ran a deer, he got so mad he beat the dogs bloody with a hickory switch when they returned.

Blood flew, dogs yelping, crying, and trying to get away from him as he tightly held onto their leashes. Slowly moving, with their tail between their legs, they crawled under the truck for cover.

* * *

I could spend a lot of time on hunting as it relates to trauma, triggers, mindlessness, and the need to self medicate.

"What are fixed Ideas? What are movable ideas? How do they serve me?"

Clifford L. Carter

SOMATIC AWARENESS

NEUTRALIZING DIS-EASE COURSE MATERIAL

(17)

FIXED & MOVABLE

WHEN CONSIDERING FIXED AND MOVABLE as the mind processes information, grasps, or averts, consider a fixed *idea* we have held on to for a very long time. Such as, a certain group of people are untrustworthy or that another group of people are hard working, and yet another group are alcoholics or drug addicted. Those ideas seem to be burnt into our psyche with little chance of altering one's perception.

On the other hand, movable ideas can be seen simply as, "Today, I like chocolate and drink coffee," and a week from now I may no longer have taste for either. It also might manifest as considering one of the above groups of people free from grasping or aversion. Meaning, our mind qualifies a group or person on a case-by-case bases.

When we become aware a fixed idea enters the mind, one way to expand past that stuck point is to observe it from an alternate view. Ask one's self how accurate our conclusion about *the idea* is and if there is any space to consider something different.

We may also question from where the fixed idea originated and ask ourself if it is valid. We can refer to the chapter on dependent origination how our past informs our present and future reality.

We might also challenge a fixed idea by shifting to the opposite of what our mind is telling us to do in that moment, while exploring the outcome. Focusing on the breath and becoming aware of sensations as explained in *Neutralizing Dis-Ease* will help to slow the mind and calm the nervous system to further enable some distance from the situation.

Nothing is inherently wrong with fixed ideas. Suffering begins when we hold on to the idea of this or that being fixed or black and white. Absolute gives no space for the mind to expand into possibilities that generate hope.

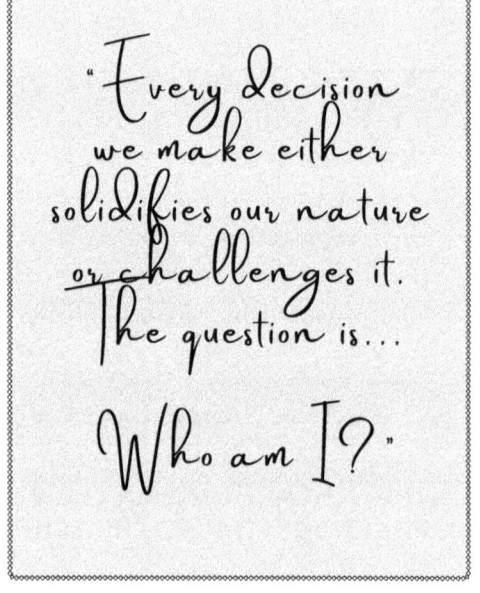

Hope, in turn, gives a way forward even if we have no idea what is at the end of the path or obstacle we must navigate.

That does not mean all thought should be movable. As in the case of a bear chasing you, a fixed idea that you are in danger and should run is helpful.

I am simply challenging fixed ideas lead to suffering when there is no space for an alternate reality.

The concept of *Enabling Dependency* is the idea that one supports another to the point the supported becomes dependent. The most prominent reason for this that underlies any given circumstance is the fear of being abandoned.

The idea one might enable another to become dependent stems from a fixed idea that "all people abandon me", and if one enables or facilitates dependency, then that person will have no other choice but to stay.

The fixed idea comes from a time in one's life when they felt they had been abandoned in some way. It might be emotionally abandoned or physically abandoned. Either way, when that becomes an identity solidified how can we manage the feelings of abandonment?

Some people who feel abandoned might find it useful to leave before the other person abandons, knowing it will happen and at the very least they will have some control as to *when* it happens.

Another strategy is to enable dependency—make themselves so needed that they believe the other person would never leave them under any circumstances.

My particular strategy with employment was to find my own way of completing a task and sell it as a much more efficient process, get others on board, then push to change systems through the organization.

I became seemingly indispensable. That, in my mind, secured a position which could not be filled by anyone else, thus eliminating any chance of being abandoned.

It was not the idea that my strategy might be helpful when one is employed but that my strategy was necessary to my feeling of safety, free from abandonment. The necessary part is also fixed and leads to pain and suffering conditioned by past experience.

"We put our own circumstances on our interactions with others, disabling our ability to set boundaries."

Clifford L. Carter

Somatic Awareness
Neutralizing Dis-Ease Course Material

(18)

Understanding Consciousness

By definition, consciousness is the awareness of self and surroundings.

Do all things experience consciousness?

I would say, "Yes, all things experience consciousness."

Human beings experience consciousness through the five senses as well as *the Thinking Mind*. Animals, insects, and all living creatures experience consciousness much the same way as human beings do. Plants experience consciousness, also.

Plants send energy up or down, depending on the season. Some plants open their flowers in the sunlight and close them at night. Plants take nutrients from the soil and water from the sky to survive and grow and even bear fruit.

Rocks and soil change over time. Some soil becomes coal and some rocks become diamonds. I believe that is also consciousness. If that is true, then the unchanging connection we human beings share with every part of our planet is *Consciousness*.

Somatic Awareness ~ Understanding Consciousness

GROWTH BY TREE...

Watching a cloudless sky matting what appears to be lifeless tree in winter. Cool breeze pushed and pulled the upward branches. I cannot help but imagine the inner growth from limbs and twigs reaching sunlight and drops of passing rain showers.

The base was so strong and rooted in its conviction and stands as a testament of strength, yet still needed so much wandering searching of its branches to even stay alive. Symbiosis, yes, with surrounding trees, and yet something even deeper within the tree itself. Yet without the nourishment of soil and water, the tree's placement would not survive in a narrow closed system.

Also without the tree's limbs and branches reaching out, risking the sun, wind, rain, cold—all the elements—tree would also never survive.

> "Childhood trauma stems the roots of great pain for generations if not weeded properly."

To gain some understanding about our own life from that tree, we must look at grounding ourselves as firmly as a tree—with nutrients for our body to sustain life.

Then, to gain understanding, truth, and wisdom, we must reach out and experience the wind, rain, sun, cold, and all the elements that foster transformation. We must reach out to fully understand ourselves. As if the outside were a mirror that exposes our true self that resides inside us.

The outside is not to justify. It is to promote questioning experience, foster learning and growth from stable foundation.

That is the lesson of tree.

* * *

"WE ARE WHO WE DECIDE TO BE"

Connecting to ourselves is the true path through trauma. Although it might be challenging and sometimes feels overwhelming, it is not a band-aid or patch.

Compassion is understanding that every experience we have is on a continuum of all experiences we have ever experienced. So to believe we were in a better place than another is truly false. We are only in a different place of understanding than we were.

The new you will always have fragments of the old you, however small. Be with, accept, and move on to, whenever, and however, they continue to arise.

SOMATIC AWARENESS

NEUTRALIZING DIS-EASE COURSE MATERIAL

(19)

TROUBLESHOOTING

As SENSATIONS ARISE, WE MIGHT be aware of the thought and action which follows time after time, enabling any given circumstance to become bigger than the ability to focus on the breath, be aware of sensation, accept sensation, and move on to the next sensation arising.

When that happens, we may or may not understand the response we have to any given attachment or even that we have become attached at all.

Simply becoming aware that it's happening can change our relationship to our response, as well as the very trigger that initiated said response.

As time goes on, being in a state of awareness more and more frequently we begin to experience overwhelming sensations as yet another seeing, tasting, touching, smelling, hearing and thinking that is awakening one to understanding how we cling to the past.

The act or action taken by responding to any sensation is necessary in understanding one's own self, and the patterning that has taken place, yet again, brings us home to the "who we have become". Again, that is an opportunity not to blame or shame ourself on how we got *here* time and time again, but a chance to be thankful we are experiencing an opportunity to self evaluate.

Is my response benefiting me in some way?

It might be necessary to look deeper or under the initial benefit by understanding our response to a sensation in any way is an indication there might be an attachment of some kind.

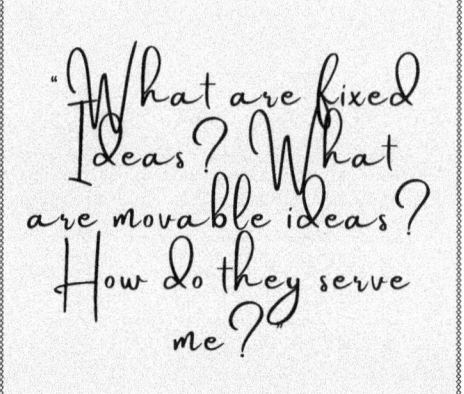

"What are fixed Ideas? What are movable ideas? How do they serve me?"

It may not be a literal attachment but simply the idea our response is necessary in the moment.

As we continue to respond and self evaluate, the benefit becomes more clear. As that happens, we then have an opportunity to ask ourself, "Is this response still working for me, or could I shift slightly to imagine a different outcome?"

Once we begin to adopt a modified response and experience the outcome, then we again are able to evaluate and modify accordingly.

By troubleshooting in this way, we continually examine ourself and our response to the world around us.

Using the tools in *Neutralizing Dis-Ease,* we slow the mind and calm the nervous system over and over, enabling us to clearly see and make adjustments as needed.

"Our dependency on rightness originated lifetimes ago, linked by the very need to feel safe."

Clifford L. Carter

Somatic Awareness

NEUTRALIZING DIS-EASE COURSE MATERIAL

(20)

Afterward

My biggest challenges have also been my biggest growth.

I've realized that only now after years of self reflection and my attempt to document my life as it unfolds through sensations followed by thought and action. I now know awakening never really comes without experience. It has been through experience and the willingness to pull myself apart that I have truly gained clarity.

That is the difficult task of inner transformation. From the inside out. Meaning that, as sensations arise, attachments become solidified, then becomes the continuous work of chipping away stone shard after stone shard to reveal what has calcified beneath. Over and over, that process seemingly never finishes. Only finding another level in need of accepting, followed by letting go.

My hope and realization with this manuscript is that some will connect and some will move onward in their journey, finding an alternative path to the 'who they have become' that might lead them to their true nature.

* * *

TWENTY QUESTIONS TO ANSWER IN THIS LIFETIME OR......?

1. LOVE

Do I have the capacity to give myself fully and completely to another?

2. HATE

Is it possible to push past all feelings and emotions when hatred arises?

3. ACCEPTANCE

After answering all nineteen questions, can I accept myself fully and unconditionally?

4. LEADER

Will I rise to the role of a leader when the time comes?

5. FOLLOWER

Can I step aside and allow another to take charge?

6. NURTURER

In times of trouble, can I compassionately align with my fellow being?

7. SPEAKER

Would I use my voice to change the world?

8. SILENCE

Can I listen to the sharing of consciousness?

9. INTROVERT

Will I go inside to find the answers to the universal questions?

10. EXTROVERT

Could I allow others to show me the way?

11. PHYSICAL PAIN

Have I gained understanding from all sources, even physical traumatic injury?

12. LONELINESS

Can aloneness become my best friend?

13. JOY

Can I feel joy so deeply I lose self?

14. EMOTIONAL SUFFERING

Can I weep so profoundly deep that my bones quiver?

15. WAR

Is my own personal war within expressing itself outwardly?

16. PEACE

Do I experience moments of calm clarity?

17. LOSS

Can losing someone bring me to my knees?

18. RAGE

Do I cling to the ideas that cause rage?

19. ENVY

Do I need to be just like_____?

20. SELF WORTH

Can I be as good as everybody else?

SOMATIC AWARENESS
NEUTRALIZING DIS-EASE COURSE MATERIAL

ABOUT THE AUTHOR

MEDITATION HAS BEEN A BIG part of my life for a very long time, learning and understanding self through the practice. Monasteries and Buddhist centers enabled me to see the world through a different lens. Immersing myself in meditation was the way back to my true nature. The obstacle to self, or true nature, was patterning. The idea that there are preset rules handed down from generation to generation fueled my need to let go of the *who I had become*. The *who I had become* was based on environmental pollutants—environmental pollutants defined as people, places, and things. This curriculum is my way of sharing the process back to self—accepting and letting go of patterning that tethers us to the *who we have become*.

Clifford L. Carter is the founder of the non-profit organization, INNER WARRIOR SPIRIT, and currently facilitates and teaches meditation practices at his Colorado property.

www.ingramcontent.com/pod-product-compliance
Lightning Source LLC
Chambersburg PA
CBHW041324110526
44592CB00021B/2817